Learning Articulate Storyline

Harness the power of Storyline to create
state-of-the-art e-learning projects

Stephanie Harnett

PUBLISHING

BIRMINGHAM - MUMBAI

Learning Articulate Storyline

First published: July 2013

Production Reference: 1190713

Published by Packt Publishing Ltd.
Livery Place
35 Livery Street
Birmingham B3 2PB, UK.

ISBN 978-1-84969-422-3

www.packtpub.com

Cover Image by Gagandeep Sharma (er.gagansharma@gmail.com)

Credits

Author
Stephanie Harnett

Reviewers
Diana D. Jaffee
Jade Kelsall
Barry Sampson
Helen Tyson

Acquisition Editor
Akram Hussain

Lead Technical Editor
Sweny M. Sukumaran

Technical Editors
Prasad Dalvi
Shashank Desai
Saumya Kunder
Larissa Pinto

Project Coordinator
Amey Sawant

Proofreader
Kevin McGowan

Indexer
Monica Ajmera Mehta

Production Coordinator
Nitesh Thakur

Cover Work
Nitesh Thakur

About the Author

Stephanie Harnett is a learning consultant who has over 20 years of training and communications experience. She has worked with business leaders, key stakeholders, and project teams, designing, developing, and delivering collaborative solutions, online learning, and interactive communications. Her areas of expertise include governance, compliance, operations, human resources in oil and gas, and government.

Stephanie is passionate about learning and technology — it is her work and her hobby. You will frequently spot her in the global community of learning professionals, sharing her knowledge through guest blog posts and tutorials. Her contributions to the community can be viewed on `stephanieharnett.ca` and by following her on Twitter (`slhice`).

Over the years, she has developed a keen awareness of adult learning in a corporate setting and uses her research and analysis, instructional design, writing, presentation, and technical skills, along with a dash of common sense, to produce effective, engaging, and on-target results that meet business challenges.

Away from the office? This is a foreign concept for Stephanie. She weaves learning and technology when she works and when she plays — finding new devices and effective ways to communicate, collaborate, work, play, learn, and share, no matter where her GPS coordinates are.

Specialties include instructional design, writing/communications, technical writing, storyboarding/layout/design, advisory, and technical support/training.

About the Reviewers

After many years in education and sales, **Diana D. Jaffee** has sidestepped into the e-learning and multimedia design arena. Always fascinated with computers and their use in education, Diana implemented teaching music theory and history in her private voice and piano studio through the use of MIDI technology and music education software.

Since starting her own e-learning development company with partner Darla Wigginton as eVision-Design, Diana has been taking PowerPoint to educational levels she never thought possible. With the release of Storyline, her goal is to find out how far she can take this technology in the world of e-learning, to provide the most effective learning possible.

Jade Kelsall has worked in higher education in the UK since she graduated in 2007. She started working in administration at the University of Leeds Library. She developed an interest in e-learning development, and soon got a position as Learning Technologist in the Skills@Library team, with a remit to develop interactive online resources to help students to develop their academic skills. While at the University of Leeds, she also worked on the EU-funded **ORCIT (Online Resources for Conference Interpreting)** project, producing interactive pedagogic tools for trainers and students of conference interpreting.

She moved to the University of Manchester Library in October 2012. Her main areas of responsibility are the design and development of a new program of innovative online resources, covering a broad range of academic skills, and to support library colleagues with the use of technology in their teaching.

Jade has also worked on a number of freelance projects in a variety of areas, including e-learning, web, and multimedia development.

Barry Sampson is a director and co-founder of Onlignment, a small consultancy with big ideas about transforming learning and development into something results focused and practical. He works with large corporates, small training companies, NGOs, charities, government agencies, and anyone else who wants to make the best use of technology to support learning and communication. In between projects, he writes and speaks on a range of topics related to learning and technology.

Occasionally, he remembers to blog at `http://barrysampson.com/`.

Helen Tyson is an experienced L&D professional and has been involved in IT training for approximately 15 years, with specific emphasis on e-learning since 2006. She has experience of training in a variety of industries, including print technology, financial services, and mail order retail.

After having used several other e-learning content development software packages, she found Articulate while working for a clinical decision support software house. This led to Helen taking part in the first ever Articulate Accredited Training for Studio 09 that took place in the UK, and she has stuck with Articulate ever since.

Currently, Helen is an e-learning consultant for Omniplex Ltd, a company that provides a comprehensive range of e-learning solutions to hundreds of organizations in the UK, Europe, and North America.

Omniplex is the only official Articulate training partner in the UK and a large part of Helen's role is to deliver Articulate Accredited Training across the UK and Europe. In addition to training, she also works on content development projects, course consultancy, and manages LMS implementations.

www.PacktPub.com

Support files, eBooks, discount offers and more

You might want to visit www.PacktPub.com for support files and downloads related to your book.

Did you know that Packt offers eBook versions of every book published, with PDF and ePub files available? You can upgrade to the eBook version at www.PacktPub.com and as a print book customer, you are entitled to a discount on the eBook copy. Get in touch with us at service@packtpub.com for more details.

At www.PacktPub.com, you can also read a collection of free technical articles, sign up for a range of free newsletters and receive exclusive discounts and offers on Packt books and eBooks.

http://PacktLib.PacktPub.com

Do you need instant solutions to your IT questions? PacktLib is Packt's online digital book library. Here, you can access, read and search across Packt's entire library of books.

Why Subscribe?

- Fully searchable across every book published by Packt
- Copy and paste, print and bookmark content
- On demand and accessible via web browser

Free Access for Packt account holders

If you have an account with Packt at www.PacktPub.com, you can use this to access PacktLib today and view nine entirely free books. Simply use your login credentials for immediate access.

Table of Contents

Preface

Storyline rocks! And you're about to discover why.

As you work through this book and get hands-on with Storyline, you'll be amazed at what you're capable of producing with little or no prior development experience, and just how quickly you can do it.

Storyline is an authoring tool packed with out-of-the-box features that don't require any special knowledge to operate. Hold on…what was that? That's right, this is a *programming-free zone* that everyone can jump into. No longer is e-learning authoring limited to developers, the doors are now wide open for subject matter experts with their content, instructional designers with their storyboards, and graphic designers with their media to work, in conjunction with developers, to collectively create some very cool e-learning projects.

Knowing this, you may want to keep it a secret and dazzle others with amazing productions that magically work on desktops and mobile devices. There will be oooo's and ahhhh's guaranteed and you will leave others impressed with how you were able to do so much, so well, and in record time.

This is a book about how to use Storyline, but it should be noted that knowing how to use Storyline features and understanding how to use Storyline for e-learning are two different things. It's like providing a guitar to someone who knows the basics. You can expect they will have mastered several chords and can play a few songs pretty well. But the same instrument with all the same features in the hands of someone such as Eric Clapton will result in something quite different. It doesn't matter how well you know Storyline, if the learning experience isn't well designed from a content point of view, you won't produce effective learning material.

The good thing about Storyline is that it isn't going to take years of training to master, like it would for an accomplished musician. It will, however, take some extra time and attention on your part to master the art of producing great results with Storyline.

Beware, Storyline is a bit like a shiny new Ferrari. It's tempting to hop in, put the pedal to the medal, and create some screaming e-learning, after all, the bells and whistles are there to use. It can be easy to go down a path that is fun, but it likely won't result in practical solutions. You'll want to keep your focus on using the features appropriately and in a way that truly helps convey a key concept or demonstrate a difficult process, or otherwise aid the learning process.

The aim of this book is to provide you with one-on-one tutoring to help you with the basics while also learning how to best apply Storyline features in the context of the work you do. When you finish this book you will confidently create shining examples of e-Learning which bring content to life in interesting and engaging ways. It is this skill that will set you apart from the crowd.

What this book covers

In *Chapter 1, Creating a Story*, you'll be introduced to the concept of a story or e-Learning course, along with a quick overview of the Storyline interface and start-up configuration tasks to prepare for creating your first story. Specifically, we'll take a look at how to create a story from scratch, how to create a new story based on a template, and how to open work you may have previously created in PowerPoint and other Articulate products.

In *Chapter 2, Adding Content into your Story*, you'll begin building the content for your first e-Learning story. To do this, you'll work with design and master slides and place a variety of content elements into your story. You'll also learn how to align, format, and animate these elements.

In *Chapter 3, Adding Interactivity*, you'll be introduced to two powerful features in Storyline: states and triggers. These features are the basis of interactive content development and you'll learn how easy it is to create basic interactions in a few simple steps.

In *Chapter 4, Adding Characters and Audio*, you'll discover how to bring story content to life by adding and editing characters. You'll also explore how to incorporate and edit audio files for sound effects and narration. You'll also learn how to add text-based captions to a story.

In *Chapter 5, Extending Slide Content*, you'll be introduced to an important concept called layers. Layers are useful in organizing content within one slide as opposed to spreading content over multiple slides. You will learn when and why you would choose to use a layer, how they work, and what's required to display layer content.

In *Chapter 6, Using Variables to Customize the Learning Experience*, you'll explore how using variables can help you create an engaging experience that responds to your learners' actions.

In *Chapter 7, Creating Learning Paths*, you'll learn about the concept of branching; re-routing a learner down a different path depending on how they respond to a question or prompt in your story. You'll learn how to create an opportunity for learner input then set up basic branching to guide the learner in a particular direction. You'll also learn how to customize slide layout to control learner navigation.

In *Chapter 8, Testing Learner Knowledge*, you'll take a first look at Storyline quizzing, including a review of a variety of quiz questions formats, and learn how you create, edit, score, and track quiz questions. You'll also learn how to import previously created quizzes from Articulate Quizmaker.

In *Chapter 9, Adding Visual Media to a Story*, you'll take a look at some seriously fun features of Storyline that allow you to add visual media such as video, screen recordings, and websites. You'll learn about supported file types along with steps for importing media and working with web objects.

In *Chapter 10, Publishing your Story*, you'll take a closer look at how a story looks when previewed and published. You'll learn about the options available to the customized colors and controls that surround your course content. Storyline supports multiple publishing outputs. The methods and the process to publish a course to the web, tablets and mobile devices full stop LMS and Word are also covered.

In *Chapter 11, Rapid development*, is about how you can easily reuse, share, and edit e-learning assets to expedite development of courses. This chapter provides some thoughts on using Storyline effectively to produce quality results while increasing your productivity.

The *Appendix*, is a collection of tutorials, links, and ideas for inspiration to help you with your Storyline skills.

What you need for this book

The first thing you need is, of course, you! Everything else is optional but a computer with Articulate Storyline installed is highly recommended. You can download a free, 30-day trial of Storyline by going to http://www.articulate.com and clicking on the **30-day free trial** button.

Who this book is for

If you're an e-Learning developer, writer, designer, subject matter expert or all or any one of these, this book is for you. It's designed to help you get up-to-speed quickly with the most useful and productive features of Storyline. You can jump into this book and glean new knowledge that will give you an edge, not just for novices, but also those of you who are seasoned developers who are transitioning from PowerPoint and Articulate Studio '09, and those who are already working with Storyline.

Conventions

In this book, you will find a number of styles of text that distinguish between different kinds of information. Here are some examples of these styles, and an explanation of their meaning.

Code words in text, database table names, folder names, filenames, file extensions, pathnames, dummy URLs, user input, and Twitter handles are shown as follows: "We can include other contexts through the use of the include directive."

New terms and **important words** are shown in bold. Words that you see on the screen, in menus or dialog boxes for example, appear in the text like this: "clicking on the **Next** button moves you to the next screen".

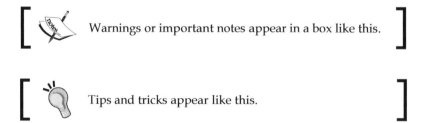

Warnings or important notes appear in a box like this.

Tips and tricks appear like this.

Reader feedback

Feedback from our readers is always welcome. Let us know what you think about this book—what you liked or may have disliked. Reader feedback is important for us to develop titles that you really get the most out of.

To send us general feedback, simply send an e-mail to feedback@packtpub.com, and mention the book title via the subject of your message.

If there is a topic that you have expertise in and you are interested in either writing or contributing to a book, see our author guide on www.packtpub.com/authors.

Customer support

Now that you are the proud owner of a Packt book, we have a number of things to help you to get the most from your purchase.

Downloading the graphics and exercises of the book

You can download the graphics and exercise files of this book from your account at http://www.packtpub.com. If you have purchased this book elsewhere, you can visit http://www.packtpub.com/support and register to have the files e-mailed directly to you.

Errata

Although we have taken every care to ensure the accuracy of our content, mistakes do happen. If you find a mistake in one of our books—maybe a mistake in the text or the code—we would be grateful if you would report this to us. By doing so, you can save other readers from frustration and help us improve subsequent versions of this book. If you find any errata, please report them by visiting http://www.packtpub.com/submit-errata, selecting your book, clicking on the **errata submission form** link, and entering the details of your errata. Once your errata are verified, your submission will be accepted and the errata will be uploaded on our website, or added to any list of existing errata, under the Errata section of that title. Any existing errata can be viewed by selecting your title from http://www.packtpub.com/support.

Piracy

Piracy of copyright material on the Internet is an ongoing problem across all media. At Packt, we take the protection of our copyright and licenses very seriously. If you come across any illegal copies of our works, in any form, on the Internet, please provide us with the location address or website name immediately so that we can pursue a remedy.

Please contact us at copyright@packtpub.com with a link to the suspected pirated material.

We appreciate your help in protecting our authors, and our ability to bring you valuable content.

Questions

You can contact us at questions@packtpub.com if you are having a problem with any aspect of the book, and we will do our best to address it.

1
Creating a Story

Let's get started!

This chapter provides a brief look at the key features of the Storyline interface, followed by the steps needed to create your first Storyline project.

Included in this book are exercises that you can follow along. To do this, you will need Internet access and Storyline installed so that you can download and work with Articulate sample templates.

In this chapter we will discuss:

- Storyline launch options and some basics about the Storyline interface
- How to create a story from scratch and from a template
- What initial settings should be reviewed before adding content to a story
- How to import existing content from PowerPoint, Articulate Engage, and Quizmaker
- How to save your first story

Downloading the graphics and exercises of the book

You can download the graphics files and exercise of this book from your account at http://www.packtpub.com. If you have purchased this book elsewhere, you can visit http://www.packtpub.com/support and register to have the files e-mailed directly to you.

Launching Storyline

Storyline presents a launch screen each time you start the program. This screen provides options for creating new projects, opening existing projects, and importing content previously created in PowerPoint or Quizmaker. You'll also find a series of helpful getting started tutorials and pre-built templates that you can download and install on your computer.

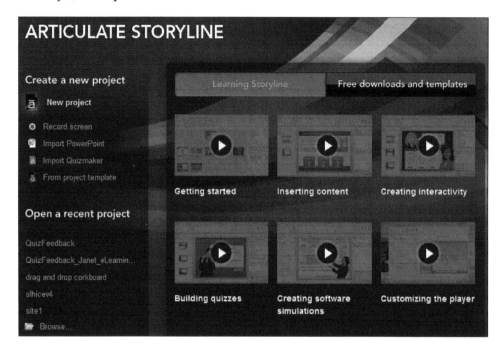

Creating a new story

You can create a new story in several ways, including the following:

- To create a new story that is devoid of content and formatting, choose the **New project** option

- To create a new story with content you previously produced in PowerPoint or Articulate Quizmaker, choose **Import PowerPoint** or **Import Quizmaker** respectively

- To create a new story where the initial content is a recording of your computer screen, choose **Record screen**

- And finally, to create a new story with Storyline template-driven content and formatting, choose **From project template**

Storyline interface

If you're following along, choose the **New project** option to create a new, blank story file. This option is best when you want to create an original story file with your own design. When **New project** is selected from the Storyline launch screen, the initial view you see looks the same as the following screenshot and contains just a single, blank slide:

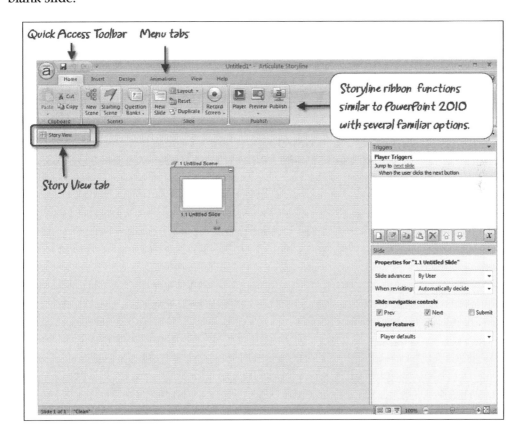

This view is called **Story View** and it's the default view.

 You can hide the ribbon by right-clicking anywhere in the ribbon and choosing **Minimize the Ribbon**. You can reveal it again by repeating this. Any item on the ribbon can be included on the quick access toolbar by right-clicking on a ribbon option and choosing **Add to Quick Access Toolbar**.

Story View

Story View is a new concept for those transitioning from Articulate Studio and one that you're likely to grow quite fond of. Story View, similar to the Slide Sorter View in PowerPoint, shows all the slides in your project, providing a big picture view of the entire project.

The following screenshot is a sample course in a Story View. You can see the slides are organized into groups. The groups are called **scenes**. Scenes help to visually organize content into logical segments similar to chapters in a book. There are no hard and fast rules of when and how to use scenes other than logical breakpoints. You could have all of your content on slides within a single scene; but as you start working with Storyline, you will appreciate the ability to group topics together.

Outside of visual organization, scenes also play a role in the menus of a project as each scene by default becomes a submenu in the navigational structure. This can be overridden of course, but by default it offers another compelling reason to use scenes; to expedite navigational refinement that is part of the publishing process.

You can clearly see from this vantage point how content flows from one slide to another. As projects become larger and more complex, you will find Story View indispensable for organizing and managing project content.

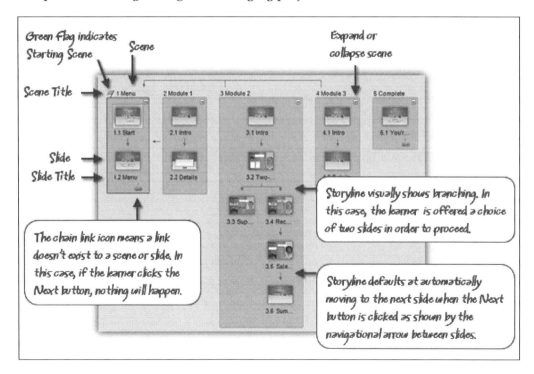

Normal View (also known as Slide View)

When working on an individual slide, you'll most often use the Normal View. This view is quite similar to PowerPoint and will be familiar to Articulate Studio users.

Normal View can be accessed in a few different ways, including the following:

- The easiest method is to double-click on the slide while in Story View
- You can switch to Normal View using the **Slide** button in the lower-right corner of the screen
- From the ribbon, you can click on the **View** tab and then choose **Normal**

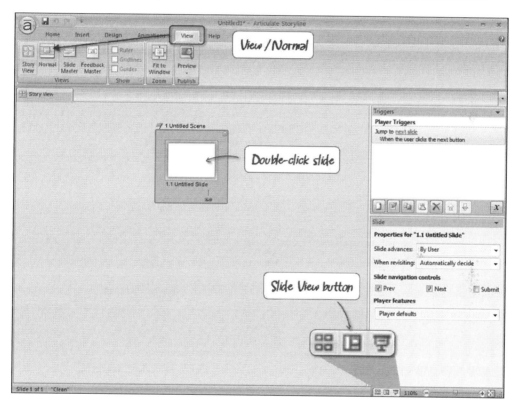

Once in Normal View, you can toggle back to Story View by clicking on the **Story View** tab, clicking on the **Story View** button, or choosing **View | Story View** from the ribbon as shown in the following screenshot:

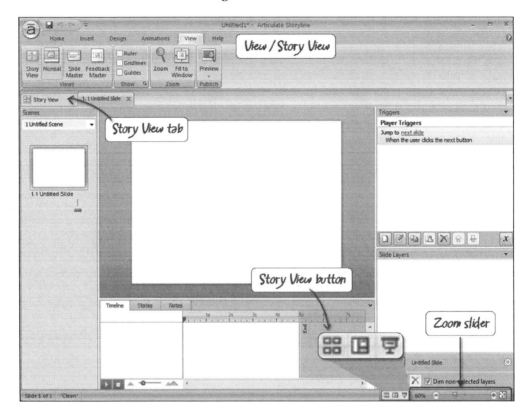

In both views, you will notice a zoom slider in the lower-right corner. You can use this to adjust the viewing size of the slide or the viewing size of the scenes and slides, depending on if you are in Normal or Story View.

The far right side of the slider displays a *fit to window* button that you may find useful to quickly fit the slide or Story View content back into the available screen space.

The slider is a quick method of controlling zoom levels. You can also do this by holding the *Ctrl* key and moving the track wheel up or down (using a mouse that has a track wheel).

Preparing a story

When you create a new story there is one thing you need to review, and ideally adjust, before adding content to your story and this is called **story size**.

Story size

The default size for a story is 720 px x 540 px. This refers to the slide size, and is the same 4:3 aspect ratio and slide size as a default PowerPoint file. The project size will be larger in dimension when published, since the player (the interface that appears around the perimeter of the slides) can consume up to 260 pixels in width and 118 pixels in height.

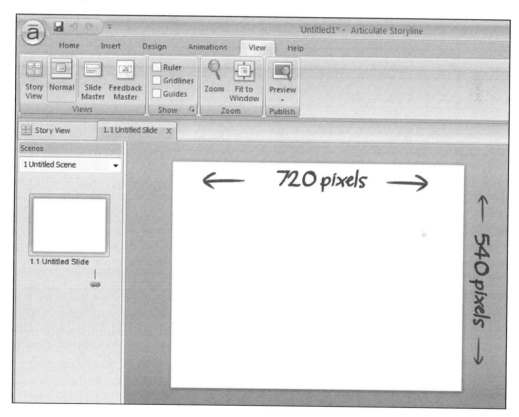

You can adjust the story size at any time, but it's best to do this before adding content. This is because existing slide content is rescaled to fit the new slide dimensions, which could result in text appearing smaller or larger than you'd like and graphics being stretched disproportionately.

Adjusting the story size

The setting to adjust the story size and the option to control it is found under the **Design** tab.

You can adjust the story size from the default to any size you'd like. The 720 px x 540 px default is a 4:3 aspect ratio, while the 720 px x 405 px preset is a widescreen 16:9 aspect ratio. If selecting a custom size, you can decide whether or not you want to lock the aspect ratio.

There are two options that you can work with to control the result of resizing, depending on whether the new size is larger or smaller than the existing story dimensions.

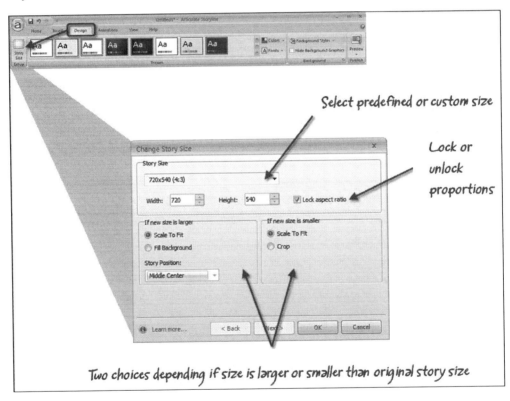

When sizing a story, you have the option to scale the contents of a slide to fit proportionately within the new size. Sometimes, scaling produces undesirable results, such as stretching images. You may opt to work with non-scaling options instead. If the size of the story is larger, you can choose to scale the background only, leaving the objects on a slide unchanged. If the size is smaller, you have the option to crop content to fit within the new size.

Here are some examples of the effects sizing has on slides with content:

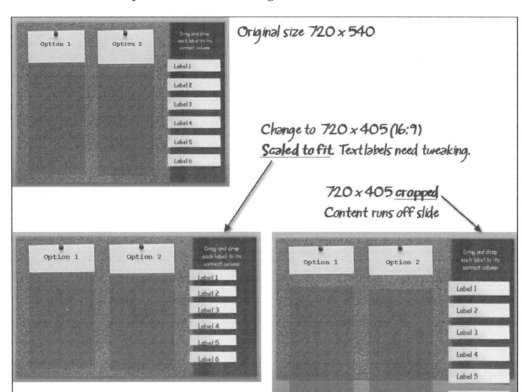

As you can see, it's possible to adjust story size when you have content on a slide, but it takes a little tweaking to get the right result. You'll save time by adjusting the size of your story to its final dimensions before you begin developing content.

Creating a story based on a template

Templates consist of one or more slides with design elements and functional elements such as animations and interactions. Storyline ships with templates that you can leverage to kick start the development of your e-learning projects.

Storyline templates have the file extension of .storytemplate and are located in **My Documents | My Articulate Projects | Storyline Templates** on your local hard drive. This folder will also contain any templates you download or create yourself.

Two templates ship with Storyline: **Character Panels** and **Top Interactions**.

There are two ways to create a story from a template:

- Choose **From project template** from the Storyline launch screen or double-click on a `.storytemplate` file in Windows Explorer to open a new story based on the template chosen.

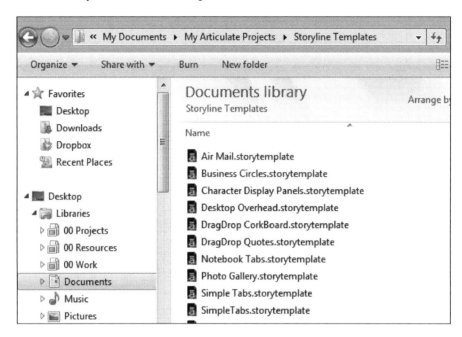

From the **Insert** tab, choose **New Slide | Templates** to add new content based on a template into an existing story and then follow these steps to insert the template's content into a story:

1. From the **Template** drop-down menu, select a template.

2. One or more slides will appear. Click to select a slide template or hold down the *Ctrl* key and click to select more than one slide template. You can also use *Ctrl + A* to select all slide templates.

3. From the **Insert into scene** drop-down menu, choose how you would like the slides to be inserted into the existing story. There are three choices:

   ○ **Current scene**: Places new slides directly after the current slide

   ○ **Same as imported template**: Inserts the slides into the current story in the same way they were originally named and organized.

   ○ **New scene**: Places the new slides into a scene of their own

4. Click on **Import**.

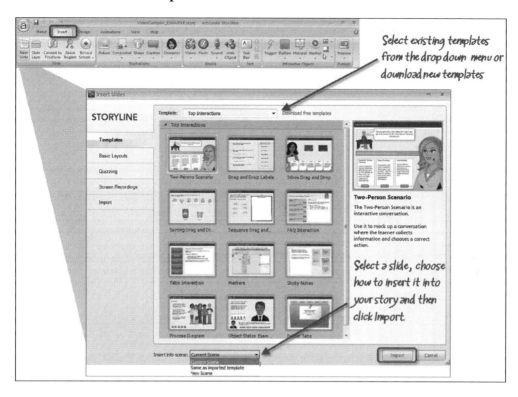

After creating a story from a template or inserting slides based on a template into an existing story, the template used will be added into your template library and will appear in the **Templates** drop-down menu the next time you use the menu.

Templates are located in **My Documents | My Articulate Projects | Storyline Templates**. You can rename templates, copy templates into this folder, or delete templates that you no longer use, just like you would with any Windows folder. Changes made here will be reflected in the **Templates** drop-down menu.

File Open versus From project template

If you choose **File | Open** to open a template, Storyline will open the template and you can make changes to the content, formatting, and interactions within the template. If you save the template, you will be overwriting the original template. If you would rather create a new story or new content from a template (as opposed to editing the formatting and functionality of a template) choose one of the two preceding methods instead.

Importing content from external sources

Storyline offers features that help you leverage work you've already done in PowerPoint, Articulate Studio '09, and even other Storyline files. Although Storyline does a very good job at accurately transitioning content from other sources, there are variances. The variances are largely related to different formatting and feature support between the products.

There are two main methods of importing content; from the launch menu at start-up or from within an open project:

- Choose **Import PowerPoint** or **Import Quizmaker** from the Storyline launch screen.
- From within an open project, select the **Articulate** menu and choose **Import**. There are more import options available here including **Engage** and **Storyline**.

Importing PowerPoint content

Importing PowerPoint content is a great time saver. You won't need to recreate your content from scratch. Articulate does not support importing from the 64-bit version of PowerPoint 2010. You will also want to ensure your version of Office has the latest updates applied.

PowerPoint and Articulate Presenter features are not 100 percent converted into Storyline using the Import feature. For example, annotations, branching, attachments, presenter bios, learning games, and player template settings are not imported (a complete and current list of considerations when importing from PowerPoint can be found on the Articulate support website at `http://www.articulate.com/support/kb_article.php?product=st1&id=catmp4tjk9r8`). Most of these features can be manually recreated after importing. It's recommended you look at the PowerPoint **Import** option as a way to bring content into Storyline more than a functionality of PowerPoint or Presenter into Storyline.

The content conversion isn't quite one to one. There are some differences you can expect as noted here:

- Some variations in font size, line spacing, alignment, colors, and bullets (Storyline doesn't support embedded PowerPoint fonts)
- If the PowerPoint presentation is of a different size to the Storyline size, some adjustments will be needed to be made in graphic and text size and alignment
- Entrance and exit animations along with emphasis and motion paths are not supported in Storyline

- Border and line thickness may appear different in Storyline
- 3D rotations and GIF images aren't supported in Storyline
- Smart Art objects, tables, and equations are imported as non-editable images

Even with features that are not 100 percent supported, you may find it faster to import content in, rather than manually replacing or manually recreating the content.

 When importing Articulate Presenter content into Storyline, you will need to make sure that the .ppta file as well as any embedded Quizmaker (.quiz) and Engage (.intr) interactions are all located in the same folder.

Selecting slides

After selecting a PowerPoint file, Storyline will display thumbnail images for all slides in the presentation. By default, all slides are selected, as indicated by a yellow border around each selected slide. You can change this by clicking on and selecting just one slide, or by using *Shift* + click or *Alt* + click, or you can select all slides again using *Ctrl* + *A*. The imported content will appear in the current scene or a new scene depending on your **Insert into scene** selection.

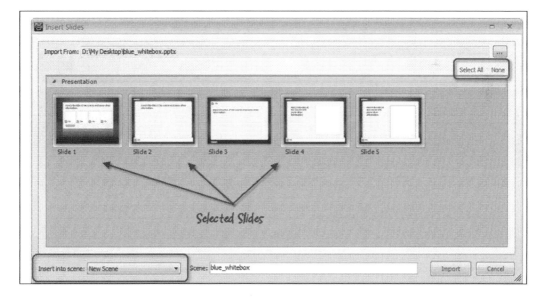

Once done, slides will appear in Storyline and you can freely edit the objects on the slides and apply formatting and functionality to them.

Importing Articulate Quizmaker content

Importing a Quizmaker file is straightforward and works well. Storyline maintains most of the original formatting and functionality, making it a snap to rapidly incorporate existing quizzes into your Storyline projects.

One consideration is that Quizmaker has a default slide size of 686 px x 424 px whereas Storyline defaults at 720 px x 540 px. For that reason, you can expect some minor formatting to tweak the alignment of text and graphics.

Articulate Quizmaker files have an extension of .quiz. After selecting a .quiz file to import, Storyline will display thumbnail images for all the slides in that quiz, divided into sections based upon the question groups they are in. As with other methods of importing, you can select one, a few, or all of the slides to import into Storyline.

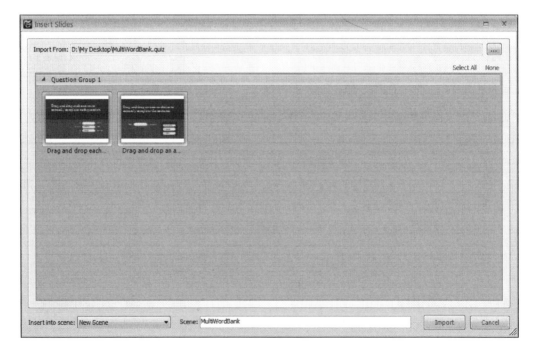

Once done, the questions, feedback, and results are 100 percent editable in Storyline.

Importing Articulate Engage content

Unlike importing PowerPoint slides and Quizmaker files, Engage conte
modified within Storyline except for resizing the interaction on the slid
modify Engage content, you must be working in Articulate Engage.

Importing Engage interactions provides the ability to playback previously created
interactions without having to rebuild them in Storyline. However, you may want to
rebuild them, as Storyline contains all of the features of Engage plus some that take
interactions to the next level in terms of look, feel, and functionality. Another reason
to rebuild them is that they are Flash interactions and Flash does not playback on
most mobile devices or the iPad.

The steps to import an Engage interaction are the same as with PowerPoint
and Quizmaker.

Importing Storyline content

This sounds unusual but it's a really neat feature of Storyline. Being able to import
Storyline files lets you combine content in a smart way; you can pick and choose
specific slides from certain project files to import. The look, feel, and functionality
are imported. This is a great feature for re-usability where you create a library of
your own interactions and layouts, then re-use them inside many different projects.

Saving a story

It won't take long to start to accumulate content in your story, especially when
working with pre-built templates or importing content from external sources. It's a
good idea to save your work often and it is recommended that Articulate files are
saved locally instead of on network drives or USB sticks, to prevent file errors.

There are three ways in which you can save your story:

- The quickest way to save your work is to press *Ctrl + S* on your keyboard. If
  this is the first time you are saving a file, you will be prompted for a filename
  and location. Subsequent presses of *Ctrl + S* will save the file under the same
  name without additional prompts.

- You can also save a project by clicking on the **Save** button on the quick access tool bar.

- You can choose the **File** menu and select **Save** or **Save As...**.

Storyline files are saved with a .story extension.

Shortcuts

Shortcut keys are a time saver. A complete listing of shortcut keys, such as *Ctrl + S* to save a story are listed in the *Appendix*.

Give it a try

Now it's your turn. This exercise gives you a chance to practice some of the key points covered in this chapter. You'll continue to build upon this example file as you progress through the book.

1. If you've been following along with the practices in this chapter you'll likely have a blank story file already open. Close this file by clicking on the **File** menu in the upper-left corner and selecting **Close**. When prompted to save, choose **Don't Save**. From the Storyline launch screen, choose **From project template**.

2. Navigate to **My Documents | My Articulate Projects | Storyline Templates**.

3. Select Character Panels.storytemplate and click **Open**.

4. Various character templates appear. Look for the one titled **Folder**, select it, and click on the **Import** button.

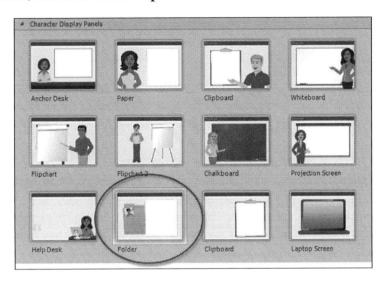

5. After the template opens, notice there is a single scene with a single slide. Both should be renamed to be more descriptive. Follow these steps:

    1. Right-click on the scene (grey boundary around the slide) and select **Rename**. Type the new name as Starting Sequence.

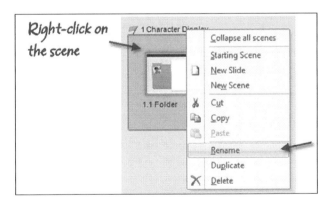

2. Right-click on the slide, select **Rename**, and type the new name as Home.

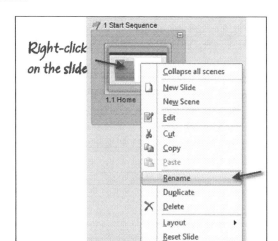

6. Click on the **Fit to Window** button to the right of the zoom slider in the lower-right corner of the scene. This will enlarge the Story View display to make content on the slide viewable.

7. Double-click on the slide to switch to Normal View.

8. Change the aspect ratio of the project to widescreen by choosing the **Design** tab and then **Story Size**. Change the size to 720 px x 405 px (16:9). Choose **Scale to fit** and click **OK**.

9. Save the story by pressing *Ctrl + S*, typing Exercise 1 - Workplace Compliance in the filename box and clicking on the **Save** button.

Summary

This chapter introduced some of the basics of the Storyline interface, including two new concepts for PowerPoint and Articulate Presenter users: Story View and scenes.

Story View is a powerful new way of looking at your project content. You can see how slides are grouped into scenes, and the navigational relationships between slides and scenes.

With these basics in hand, including configuring story size, working with templates, and importing content from external sources, you're now ready to add text and images into your story and make it sparkle and shine using Storyline formatting and animation techniques.

2
Adding Content into your Story

When you begin a new project in Storyline, you are presented with a single scene and a single blank slide within the scene. Think of this as a blank canvas; one that you design and configure in any way you see fit to create an awesome learning experience for those taking your course.

That said, not everything you create will need to be a one-off original that begins with a blank canvas; there are always constraints of time and budget that limit how far you can take things. Storyline's built-in templates, while not the focus of this chapter, will be leveraged in the exercises in this chapter, to quickly add content to your story so that you can focus your effort on customizing rather than creating from scratch.

In this chapter you will learn:

- How to work with the Timeline
- How to insert and format slide content
- More about working with slides and Story View
- To control the design of your story through master slides, backgrounds, colors, and fonts
- How to animate objects on a slide and animate transitions between slides
- To use the **Preview** function to see how your slides look and function

Working with the Timeline

The **Timeline** lists all of the objects, or content, that is present on a slide and is used to arrange and animate objects as well as control slide duration.

The **Timeline** tab appears in the **Timeline**, **States** and **Notes** panel directly below the slide when in **Normal View** as shown below:

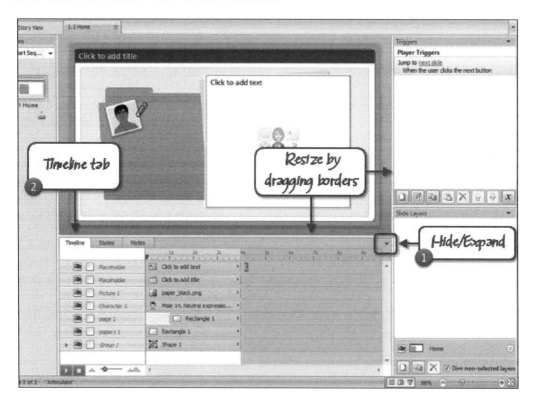

If you can't see the Timeline, then perform the following steps:

1. Click on the small arrow in the lower-right corner of the slide stage to display the **Timeline**, **States**, and **Notes** panel.
2. Click on the **Timeline** tab to display the Timeline.

The Exercise 1 – Workplace Compliance file, created in *Chapter 1, Creating a Story*, contains a combination of text, graphics, and placeholder content. A listing of the slide objects appears in the Timeline, as shown in the previous image.

Here are a few things you should know when working with the Timeline:

- You can turn the visibility of objects on or off. You may find yourself doing this when objects are positioned in similar locations on the slide and you want to edit an object that appears beneath another. Temporarily turning the visibility of the top object off lets you clearly see the bottom object. You'll need to remember to turn visibility back on as objects that are not visible also do not appear in your final, published course.

- You can rename objects and should get into the habit of doing this. Creating short, meaningful names will help you clearly identify what the object is. In the next screenshot, renaming the first **Placeholder** object to be Intro Text makes it more obvious what kind of object it is and what it contains.

- You can also lock objects. This is a handy feature to prevent accidental movement or formatting of objects that you do not want to change:

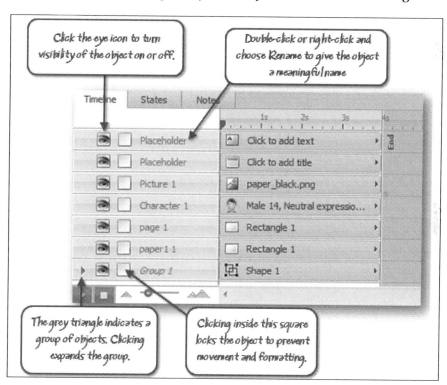

Controlling the appearance of objects

The order of objects is important. Storyline overlaps slide objects so that the object at the top of the list in the Timeline is in front of all other slide objects.

You can move objects to a different stacking order by clicking on the object directly in the timeline and dragging it up (bring forward) or down (send backward). You can also right-click on an object on the slide and choose the action you want to perform:

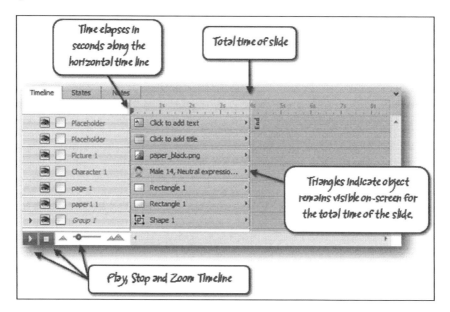

Follow along...

With the `Exercise 1 - Workplace Compliance` file open, try turning the display on and off for a few objects and note how the slide content changes. Try moving **Character 1** below **Group 1**. Notice that it disappears since it's now beneath the image of the folder. Move **Character 1** back up such that it is above **page 1**.

Reading the Timeline

The Timeline can be read vertically for stacking order and horizontally for timing. The numbers running horizontally along the top show the running time of a slide in seconds. In the example above, all slide objects are visible when the slide starts and each stays visible until the end of the slide, in this case 4 seconds.

You can quickly preview a slide by clicking on the **Play** button in the lower-left corner of the Timeline. If you want to playback from a specific point, drag-and-drop the red icon (playhead) that appears on the upper-left side of the Timeline to the point in the Timeline where you would like to start playback, and then click on **Play**. You can also **Stop** playback and use **zoom controls** to control the Timeline display. Note that during slide play back, you will not be able to interact with any of the objects.

Follow along...

Continuing with the Exercise 1 - Workplace Compliance file, let's now add some text and adjust object names and timing:

1. From the **Design** tab in the ribbon, select **Story Size** and adjust the size back to a 4:3 ratio by choosing **720 x 540 (4:3)** from the story size drop-down list.

2. Switch to **Normal View**, click in the title area where it says **Click to add title**, and type the new title as Introduction to Comstar Compliance Program.

3. It's a good habit to rename objects on a slide to something descriptive as you go along. In the Timeline, double-click on object names and rename as follows:

   ○ **Textbox** : title
   ○ **Placeholder** : introduction
   ○ **Picture 1** : paper clip
   ○ **Character 1** : employee
   ○ **Page 1** : intro paper
   ○ **Paper 1** : paper
   ○ **Group 1** : folder

4. Use your mouse to click-and-drag each object so that the timing of the object when it appears on the slide looks like the following:

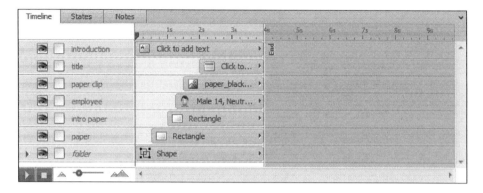

5. Click on the **Play** button to play the Timeline.

6. Save this file under a new name, `Exercise 2 - Workplace Compliance`.

Inserting content into a slide

Inserting shapes, text, and other objects onto a slide is similar to when using Microsoft Word, Excel, or PowerPoint. For example, to add a rectangle shape to a slide, select the **Insert** tab and click on the **Shape** option to choose a rectangle shape, and click-and-drag the slide to insert, position, and size the rectangle.

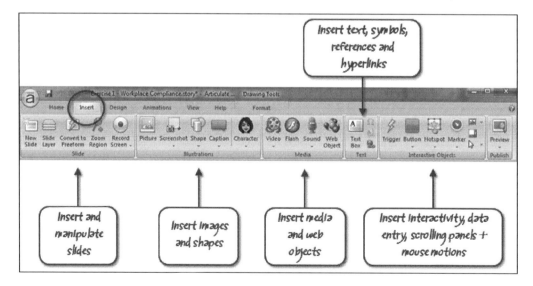

Once you have objects, images, text, or other content on a slide, you can format them in a familiar way as you would with Microsoft Office products:

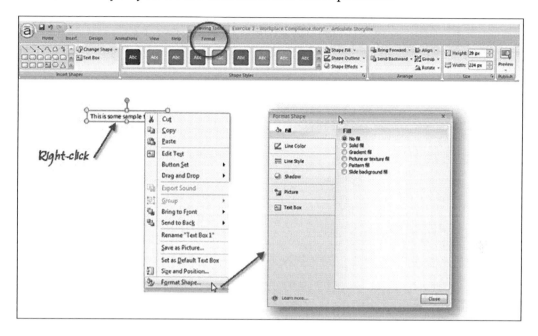

You also use familiar mouse gestures when working with slide objects:

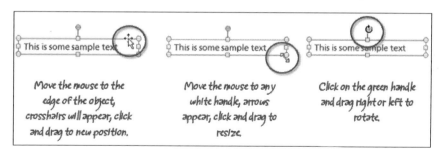

Here are some common adjustments you might make to a Storyline shape:

- **Change Shape**: This is handy if you'd like to change an object to another shape, for example, a textbox that is a box into a circle.

- **Quick Styles**: This is an easy way to change the fill color, font, outline, and effect of a shape. The color choices depend on the current design theme (design themes are covered in more detail later in this chapter).

- **Shape Fill, Outline, and Effects**: You can fill a shape with a solid or semi-transparent fill color, picture, gradient, or texture. You can also add a line around a textbox of various colors, widths, and styles.

- **Shape Effects**: This can add shadows, reflections, glows, and soft edges.

 The **Format Painter** is a handy feature found on the **Home** tab, making it easy to apply formatting from one object to another. Select the object whose format you wish to apply, click on **Format Painter** and then click on the object to format. You can also double-click on the **Format Painter** to apply formatting to multiple objects.

Grouping objects

You can group objects together to help with slide organization. For example, if five objects make up the image of a folder, you can group those objects together and name the group as "file folder". In that way all objects related to the folder are kept together.

To group objects, select all of the objects to be grouped by drawing an outline around them on the slide or shift-clicking to select multiple objects. Then press *Ctrl + G* or right-click and select **Group**.

 You can quickly select all objects on a slide by pressing *Ctrl + A*.

Follow along...

Let's turn back to Exercise 2 – Workplace Compliance, this time the focus will be on editing and adding objects to the slide:

1. Click on the text placeholder, where it says **Click to add text**. Type =lorem() and then press *Enter*. This is a quick way to insert sample text into a textbox.

2. Resize the employee image to make it large and then, while the image is selected, click on the green handle above the image to rotate it so that the image appears straight. Now let's move it so that it looks similar to the following screenshot:

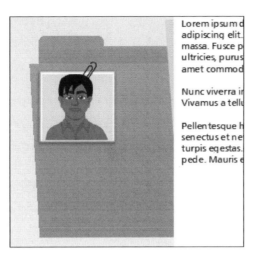

3. Refine the look of the employee image by adding an **Offset Diagonal Bottom Left shadow** to it.

4. Select the employee and the paper clip and group them by pressing *Ctrl + G*.

5. Rename this group from **Group 1** in the Timeline to employee.

6. Insert a textbox below the employee image and type Compliance Matters!

7. Rename this textbox from **Text Box 1** to be compliance matters.

8. Adjust the width of the box to go from edge to edge of the visible portion of the folder image changing the font to **Articulate Extrabold**, the size to **18pt** and alignment to be centered.

9. Insert a rectangle shape and draw it so it goes across the white part of the slide and make it tall enough to cover the words Compliance Matters!

10. Right-click on the rectangle, choose **Format Shape** and change the following attributes:

    ° Change the **Shape Fill to** black.

    ° Turn the **Shape Outline** off by selecting **No Outline**.

    ° Change the slide **Transparency** to 60 percent. Click on **Close** when done.

11. Rename **Rectangle 1** to be `compliance box`.

12. Move the `compliance box` so that it is centered over the words **Compliance Matters!**

 For precise alignment, select the words **Compliance Matters!** and for the rectangle navigate to **Align | Middle** from the **Format** tab.

13. Select the words **Compliance Matters!** then change the font to a lighter color.

14. Move the words **Compliance Matters!** above the compliance box in the Timeline.

15. Select `compliance matters` and `compliance box` then group them.

16. Rename the new group titled **Group 1** to be `subtitle`.

17. Move the `subtitle` group below `intro paper` in the Timeline.

18. Move the `subtitle` group to begin at the 2.5 seconds mark in the Timeline.

19. Save the file:

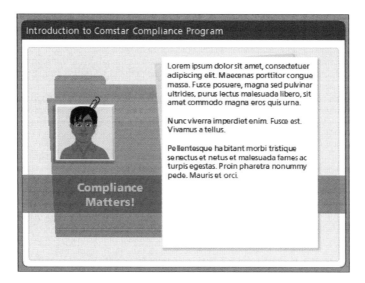

Working with text

By now you've seen that inserting, sizing, and formatting text objects in Storyline is similar to with PowerPoint and other Microsoft Office products. There are two features in Storyline that provide additional functionality to text in your story:

Scrolling panels

A scrolling panel lets you place a large volume of text (or just about any other object) that would normally consume a lot of space on a slide, into a contained area. If the text overflows, the learner will be able to scroll vertically and horizontally to see all of the information. You can have as many scrolling panels on a single slide as you like.

To create a scrolling panel, choose the **Insert** tab from the ribbon and then select **Scrolling Panel**.

Slide notes

If you've used Articulate Presenter you will be familiar with slide notes. Storyline handles this the same way, allowing you to add notes to each slide. Notes can be viewed in the published story as transcripts, narration captions, or instructions.

To add slide notes, click on the **Notes** tab in the **Timeline**, **States**, and **Notes** panel. You can format notes using most of the text and paragraph formatting options including fonts, bullets, and alignment.

The following screenshot provides examples of scrolling panels and slide notes:

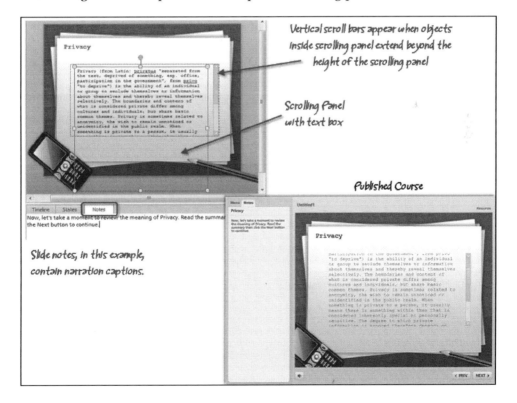

Working with pictures and screenshots

You can insert a picture from your computer or a screenshot using Storyline's built-in screenshot tool.

 Storyline does not have a clipart feature like PowerPoint. To work with Microsoft clipart, download the images needed from http://office.microsoft.com/en-us/images/ and insert them into Storyline.

Inserting a screenshot

Storyline's screenshot tool lets you capture images from other applications that are running on your computer or any portion of the screen.

Here's how to add screenshots:

1. While viewing a slide, click on the **Insert** tab and choose **Screenshot**.
2. A drop-down list appears displaying all open applications or windows on your computer. Minimized applications or windows will not appear on the list.
3. Move the mouse over any thumbnail in the list to see the application or window name and click to insert a screenshot of that item into the current slide.
4. To take a screenshot of just a portion of the screen, choose **Screen Clipping** instead. Storyline will temporarily disappear to allow you to click-and-drag the mouse to select the area of the screen to be clipped. The selected area will not be dim. Just release the mouse to insert the screenshot into the current slide.

Adjusting the properties of pictures and screenshots

Similar to adjusting the way a textbox or shape appears, you can apply graphic treatments to images. These are similar to the options in PowerPoint, though not quite as many:

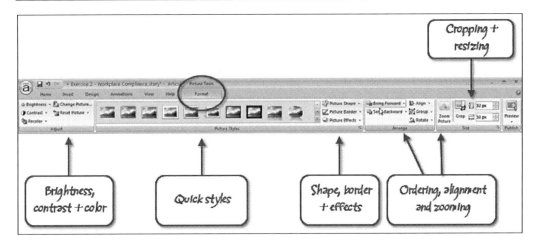

It's fairly common practice to edit your images in a tool other than Storyline, however, if you don't have another image editing tool or just need to make a few minor adjustments, here are some things you can do:

- Touch up a picture by adjusting brightness, contrast, and color.
- Add a cool picture style. This is an easy way to alter the look of an image without any fuss.
- Change the shape of a picture to create interesting effects.
- Add a border.
- Jazz up a picture by adding shadows, reflections, glows, and soft edges.

You can let learners zoom up an image, which is particularly useful for more complex graphics, flowcharts, and diagrams. You can do this by selecting the image, and choosing **Format | Zoom Picture**.

Visual help

When working with objects on a slide, like a textbox or other shape, it's a good practice to turn on visual guidance to assist with positioning and alignment. There are three tools available that can be toggled on or off by right-clicking on the outside area of the slide or from the **View** tab in the ribbon:

- **Ruler**: This displays vertical and horizontal rulers in the slide stage area.

- **Guidelines**: This displays rows and columns of dotted lines, each eight pixels wide, creating a grid. This can be adjusted by expanding the **Show** option.

- **Guides**: This is a vertical and horizontal guide which appears initially in the center of the slide, however, you can use the mouse to click-and-drag these guides into position and *Ctrl* + click to create new ones.

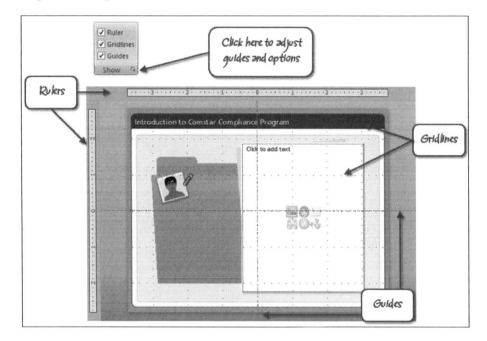

 By default, when you move an object around a slide it will align itself to the nearest gridline even if gridlines aren't turned on. While this is usually helpful, it can occasionally interfere with the precise alignment of objects. You may opt to temporarily turn this feature off. You can do this from the **View** tab, expanding the **Show** option (under Ruler, Gridlines, and Guides) and turning off the checkmark beside **Snap objects to grid**.

Working with slides

It's easy to expand content in your story by inserting new slides. You can do this from the **Insert** tab by selecting **Insert Slide**.

There will be several options; in each case click on the thumbnail image in the template, basic layouts, quizzing, screen recordings, or import to insert a slide into the project.

You have control over how this is inserted; into the current location in the current scene, in the same way as how it is set up in the template (it can be a single slide or a slide within a scene) or as a slide in a new scene in the existing project.

Here's a brief description of each **Insert New Slide** options:

- **Templates:** These are a great way to leverage and reuse content. There are templates that come pre-packaged with Storyline, templates that can be downloaded from the Articulate community, or templates that you've created.

- **Basic Layouts:** These show options that are available based on existing Slide Masters and slide layouts within the project that's currently open. Storyline comes with default layouts that you can customize or you can create your own new layouts.

- **Quizzing:** This lets you insert a graded question, a survey question, or one of the several freeform-style interactions.

- **Screen Recordings:** These let you insert a simple movie of your screen that shows learners how to perform a task or an interactive video that learners can interact with to try or test their knowledge.

- **Import:** This is used to bring in content from an existing PowerPoint file, an Articulate Quizmaker quiz, an Articulate Engage interaction, or another Storyline project as covered in *Chapter 1, Creating a Story*.

 If you have a slide that has objects and formatting you'd like to use elsewhere in your story, you can duplicate the slide by selecting the slide and pressing *Ctrl + D* to duplicate or you can also use copy and paste to achieve the same.

Organizing slides in Story View

Once there are a few slides in your story, you can switch to Story View by clicking on the **Story View** tab or choosing the **View** tab then selecting **Story View**.

Scenes and slides are automatically numbered in Story View. This numbering system is dynamic and will update depending on where a slide or scene is positioned. Slide numbering and scene numbering does not affect when navigational structure.

From **Story View** you can see a bigger picture of all the slides in the story and can begin to organize and arrange the slides within a scene, or create multiple scenes to group related slides together similar to how you group multiple objects on a slide:

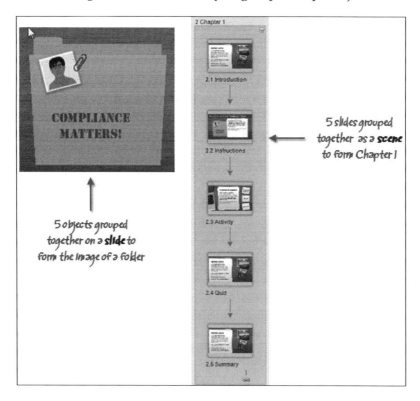

To move slides within a scene in Story View:

1. Click on the slide you wish to move (a yellow box will appear around the selected slide).

2. Click-and-drag the slide into the position in the scene where you would like it to appear.

To create a new scene in Story View, click on the **Home** tab then select **New Scene**.

To expand and collapse scenes, click on the minus or plus icon on the right-hand side of the scene to expand or collapse a scene.

Here is how we set the starting scene:

The **starting scene** in Storyline is the scene that begins an e-learning project; the very first thing the learner sees. The starting scene is indicated in **Story View** by a green flag. You can control which scene is the starting scene by right-clicking on the scene and by choosing **Starting Scene**.

Follow along...

Let's continue with Exercise 2 - Workplace Compliance, this time the focus will be on expanding the course, organizing slides, and customizing content. The first step in the process is to add new slides into the story to expand each of the compliance topics. You will work with a prebuilt Articulate template to do this (note that you will need to sign up for a free Articulate community forums account to download the template):

1. Select the **Insert** tab and choose **New Slide**.

2. Click on the **Templates** tab and click on the down arrow in the Template drop-down list to view the existing templates you have installed. If **Desktop Overhead** is not listed, click on the **Download free templates** link. This will open the browser and direct you to the Articulate template download site located at http://community.articulate.com/downloads/g/storyline/default.aspx.

3. From the template site, click on **Desktop Overhead** and then on the **Download this file** link. When asked to open or save the file, choose **Open**. The **Desktop Overhead** template now appears in your templates list.

If you encounter problems opening the template, choose to save it instead when downloading from the Articulate site. Open the location in Windows Explorer where the template was saved and copy the 1-DesktopOverhead.storytemplate file to the Storyline templates folder on your computer (\My Articulate Projects\Storyline Templates).

4. The **Desktop Overhead** template contains five slide layout variations. Select the **Benefits** slide. Click on **Import** to insert a new slide based on this template.

5. Rename this slide as Menu and then work within the slide to remove some of the interactivity (you will recreate this in the subsequent exercises):

    ° Select the three yellow post-it notes and delete them.

    ° There are three layers in the **Slide layers** pane on the right-hand side of the screen. You won't be needing these right now so let's remove them (we will go into more detail regarding layers in the subsequent chapter). Click on the layer titled **Tab 1** and then click on the red **X** icon to remove the layer. Select **Yes** to confirm. Repeat the steps for **Tab 2** and **Tab 3**:

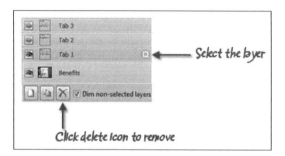

6. Save the file.

7. Click inside the textbox that displays the words **Bonus Plus** and rename it as Welcome to Comstar!

8. In the Timeline, rename the first textbox as Introduction and the second as Welcome.

9. Select all of the text inside the Introduction textbox and replace with =lorem(). Delete the last two paragraphs to shorten the volume of sample text.

10. Recreate the post-it notes by performing the following steps:

    1. Insert a rectangle of the size of the previous post-it notes. Format it as follows:

    2. Change the **Shape Fill** option to **yellow**, the **Shape Outline** option to **No Outline**, and add an **Offset Diagonal Bottom Right shadow** under **Shape Effects**.

    3. Type Business Conduct as the name to appear on the note. Change the font color to **Black**, size to **18pt**, and font to something casual like **Comic Sans**.

4. Rename the rectangle from **Rectangle 1** to Business Conduct.

5. Duplicate the note two times by selecting the note and pressing *Ctrl + D* twice or holding down the *Ctrl* key, clicking the mouse then dragging two times. Align the copies vertically on the right-hand side of the slide. Change the second note to be renamed as Privacy and the third note to be renamed as Security.

6. Select the three notes, click on the **Format** tab, and navigate to **Align | Distribute Vertically**. Now choose **Align Left**:

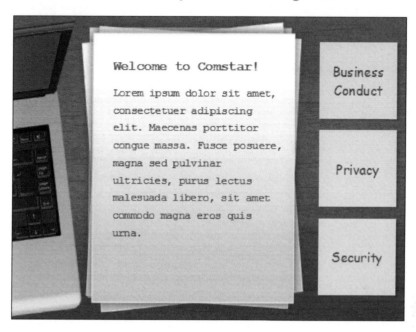

11. Insert two new slides by selecting the **Insert** tab and choosing **New Slide**. From the **Desktop Overhead** template, select the **Welcome** and **Objectives** layouts.

12. Rename the first Welcome slide to Business Conduct and make the following changes:

    1. Change the title of **Welcome to Comstar** to Business Conduct.

    2. Select all of the text below the title and replace it with =lorem().

    3. Add a screenshot and picture zoom by performing the following steps:

4. Open your browser, go to Google and search for **corporate privacy definition**. Keep the browser open (do not minimize it) and switch back to Storyline.

5. Select the **Privacy** slide.

6. Click on the **Insert** tab and then navigate to **Screenshot | Screen Clipping**.

7. The Storyline window disappears temporarily and the desktop dims. You should see the browser with the search results. Click and draw a box around a small portion of the results and release the mouse.

8. You will return to Storyline with an image of the screen. Resize and move the image to the upper-right corner.

9. Click on the image and click on the **Format** tab.

10. Add a **picture style** to the image (whatever you think looks best) and then click on the **Zoom Picture** command. This will enlarge the picture when the user clicks on it:

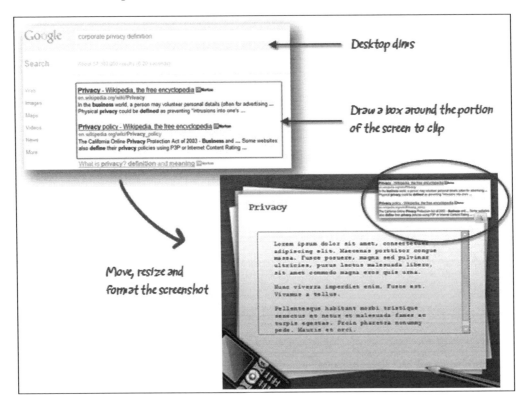

13. Rename the second **Welcome slide** to `Privacy` and make the following changes:

    1. Change the title from **Company Overview** to `Privacy`.

    2. Delete the image of people and the click to view video note.

    3. Add a scrolling textbox to display longer segments of text. To do this, perform the following steps:

    4. Click on the **Insert** tab and then on **Scrolling Panel**.

    5. Draw an area in the middle of the page, where the scrolling panel will appear (similar to the screenshot above).

    6. Insert a new textbox making it about half the width of the slide and type `=lorem()` to fill with sample text. Press *Enter* a couple times after the first sample text ends and type `=lorem()` again so that you have lots of text.

    7. Drag the textbox and release it inside the area drawn as a scrolling panel. You'll notice that the scroll bars appear. These can be used to scroll up and down through this section of the text.

14. Rename the last slide to `Security` and make the following changes:

    1. Change the title from **Course Objectives** to `Security`.

    2. Resize and center the title so that it fits within the yellow paper.

Images and objects that extend beyond the slide are not visible when previewing or publishing, such as the paper images on this slide. You could take the extra step of cropping to fit the image within the slide area to prevent the screen from shifting up and down when editing.

3. Replace the text underneath the title to `=lorem()` removing the last paragraph as this goes off slide and is not needed:

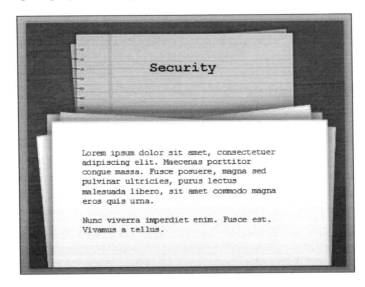

15. Switch to Story View to see how the flow of the course is shaping up. Switch back to Normal View when done and save the file.

Customizing slide design

Storyline offers several features to help you customize the design of your project. Templates such as the Desktop Overhead come with specific colors, fonts, backgrounds, and slide layouts. All of these components can be edited to enable you to create your own unique variation or you can create your own original template from scratch.

Here are three features useful for customizing slide design:

Slide Masters

Storyline **Slide Masters** function the same way as they do in PowerPoint and they can save a lot of time by eliminating unnecessary duplication of effort. The idea of a Slide Master is that you can design and build content and activities you know will be used for multiple slides and you do this just once in the Slide Master. You then apply that master layout to one or more slides in the story. When a change is needed, instead of editing multiple slides, all you need to do is edit once in the master slide and let Storyline apply this to all slides that are using that master layout.

There can be one or more Slide Masters containing a number of slide layouts for a single course. Each layout can be edited using all the regular formatting commands.

Slide Masters can be accessed by clicking on the **View** tab and selecting **Slide Master**:

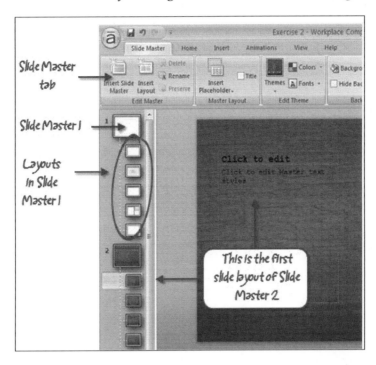

Slide Masters can consist of placeholder content. A placeholder can be set up to accept text, pictures, illustrated characters, movies, Flash, or web objects. Placeholders can be formatted and positioned using all the standard formatting functions. When a slide is using a master layout that contains a placeholder, a dotted border will appear prompting you to enter text, insert an image, and so on.

Here's how to access and work with Slide Masters:

1. From the **View** tab, choose **Slide Master**.

2. Format the master slide and layouts as you normally would for a slide.

3. Add a placeholder by clicking on the **Slide Master** tab and selecting **Insert Placeholder**. Select the type of placeholder and then use your mouse to draw and position the placeholder on the slide. You can resize and move the placeholder into position and apply formatting to it using the **Format** tab.

4. Return to **Normal View** and then right-click on a slide to which you would like to apply a master layout. To do this, choose **Layout** from the menu and select the appropriate layout.

Design themes and backgrounds

Storyline design themes and backgrounds function like they do in PowerPoint. Design themes specify colors and fonts that can be applied to one or more slides and include several built-in themes. You can choose to use the theme as it is or you can alter it to suit your needs by adjusting fonts, colors, and background styles.

Design themes, backgrounds, colors, and fonts can be accessed from the **Design** tab and can be applied to a single slide, multiple slides, or all slides.

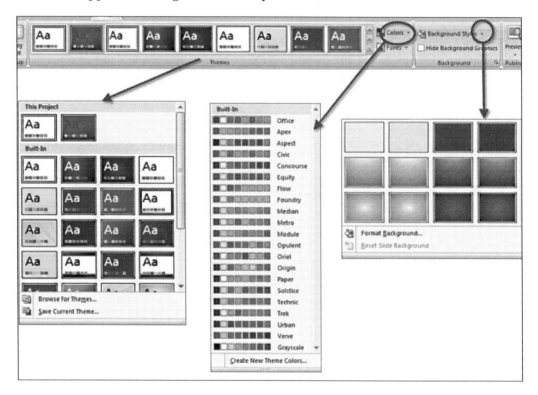

Clicking the down arrow to the right of the **Theme** list expands the list and displays options to browse and save themes. You can browse for Storyline theme files (files ending in .theme) that are not located in the default Storyline themes directory. This is useful if you share themes with others on a network or want to import a theme built by someone else. You can also save a theme under a new name if you altered the theme fonts, colors, or backgrounds and wish to keep the original intact. The new theme will appear in the **Theme** list so that it can be used in any Storyline project.

Follow along...

Working with `Exercise 2 - Workplace Compliance`, perform the following steps to apply the theme and master formatting of your sample course:

1. Select the first slide, **1.1 Home**.

2. Click on **Slide Master** and right-click on the second Slide Master (a number 2 appears next to it) and rename it as `Desktop`.

3. Hover over the fourth layout in this Slide Master. The name of the layout should display as **Custom Layout**. Click on it to select this layout.

4. Change the font for the title placeholder to be white and make this bold.

5. Exit the Slide Master, right-click on the first slide, choose **Layout** from the menu, and select **Custom Layout** from Slide Master 2.

6. Adjust the wording **Compliance Matters!** such that it's split over two lines and the font color is white.

7. Save the file.

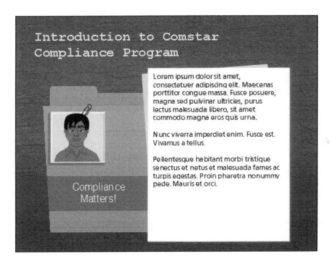

Adding animations and transitions

Storyline includes entrance and exit animations that are a subset of what is available in PowerPoint. Animations are easy to add to any object on a slide and are useful for creating emphasis and subtle motion to slide content. This is particularly true when used in combination with **Slide Transitions** that animate the transition from one slide to another using a variety of video-like effects.

Animations are fun but practice restraint when it comes to using animations in your e-learning courses. With fonts, colors, and sounds, a little goes a long way. You'll want to use these animations strategically and sparingly for greatest professional emphasis and effect.

Slide Transitions can be accessed from the **Animations** tab in Normal and Master Slide Views. Animations cannot be accessed from Story View.

Here's how to add an animation to an object on a slide:

1. Select the object you wish to animate.

2. Click on the **Animation** tab.

3. Choose an **Entrance Effect** (there are 5 different effects to choose from).

4. Choose a **Speed** (Storyline defaults at Medium but this can be adjusted).

5. Choose a direction the animation should **Enter From**. By default the animation appears from the current location but you can change this to animate in from one of eight specific directions.

6. You can repeat this process for the **Exit Animation** if you want the object to disappear off the slide in an animated fashion.

7. You can further refine when and how long an object appears on the slide using the Timeline to adjust the start and the end duration of an object.

Remember that you cannot see if animations have been applied to an object from the Timeline. You will need to select the object, and then the **Animation** menu to view animation effects. You can play the Timeline to quickly see an effect by clicking on the **Play** button in the lower-left corner of the timeline. You can also **Preview** the slide which will be covered in the next topic.

Here's how to apply a transition to a slide:

1. In Story View or Normal View, select the slide to which you want to apply a transition effect (you can only set entrance effects for slide transitions).

2. Click on the **Animation** tab.

3. Choose from one of the available **Transitions** listed in the ribbon or click on the down arrow to expand the effects list.

4. Choose a **Speed** for the transition.

5. Click on the **Apply to All** button if you wish to apply this transition effect to all slides.

6. Repeat the process for each slide where you want to apply a transition.

 You can apply animations and transitions to slide layouts and objects in layouts from the Slide Master. This can help create consistency of effects in your course.

Previewing your work

Once there are a few slides in place, you may wish to take a quick look at how things are shaping up. You can preview the current slide the current scene of or the entire story (shortcut key is *F12*) by clicking on the **Preview** button from the **Home** tab.

Previewing not only shows the slide content but also shows the default navigation including next and back buttons and the menu. Though the buttons and options are there, some may not work if you are previewing a single slide. For example, the next button will not display the next slide. This would only happen if you are previewing a scene or the entire project.

Preview shows the **Player** interface surrounding the slide content. This can be customized by changing colors, fonts, and options such as menu visibility, location, and volume control. Customizing the Player is covered in *Chapter 10, Publishing your Story*

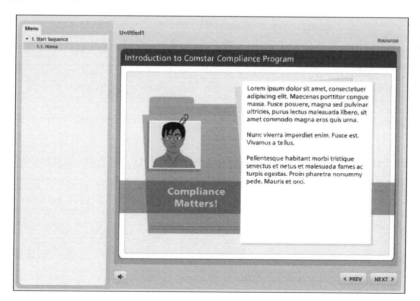

Follow along...

This last exercise will finalize our first draft of Exercise 2 - Workplace Compliance. Perform the following steps to add animations and transitions to the course:

1. Navigate to the first slide and expand the Timeline to see all objects.

2. Add the following animations:

   1. Add a **Fade In** entrance animation to the folder group.

   2. Add a **Fly In** entrance animation, and select the **Fast** speed from the **Bottom** to the intro paper.

   3. Add a **Fade In By First Level Paragraph** option from the **Top** entrance animation to the introduction.

   4. Add a **Grow In** entrance animation to the employee group.

   5. Click on the triangle besides the subtitle group in the Timeline to expand it. Click on compliance box then add a **Fade In from the Left entrance** animation and **Fade Out to the Right** exit animation.

3. **Preview** this slide. You can click on **Replay** to watch again. Click on **Close Preview**.

4. Select the **1.2 Menu** slide.

5. Adjust the color of the post-it notes and practice using **Format Painter** by following these steps:

   1. Select the first note, right-click on it and choose **Format Shape**.

   2. In the **Fill** section, click on the **Color** drop-down list and choose **More Colors**.

   3. Drag the color slider on the right-hand side of the screen higher to make the yellow a fainter color or enter 255 for Red, 255 for Green, and 110 for Blue in the respective boxes and click on **OK**, then **Close**.

   4. While the first note is still selected, click on the **Home** Tab and select **Format Painter** (or click the paintbrush icon). Click on the second note to apply the formatting. Repeat this for the third note.

6. While still on the **1.2 Menu** slide, click on the **Animations** tab and assign the **Cover Up** Slide Transition to this slide.

7. Select the last three slides and assign the Slide Transition of **Fade Out**.

8. Preview and view each slide by pressing the **Next** button in the lower-right corner of the slide. Make sure that you see the scrolling textbox and zoom screenshot on the **Privacy** slide and navigate using the menu on the left. When done, close Preview.

9. Separate each of the topic areas into a scene on its own. This helps to keep the topic areas organized, particularly as more slides are created:

    1. Switch to **Story View** and click on **New Scene** from the **Home** tab.

    2. Rename the new scene as `Business Conduct`.

    3. Repeat the steps above for Privacy and Security.

    4. Click-and-drag the **1.3 Business Conduct** slide into the new Business Conduct scene. Repeat this for each of the other two topics.

    5. Delete each of the blank slides in each new scene. The story should now look like the following screenshot. Be sure to save the file.

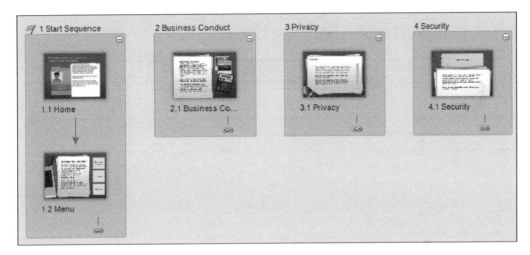

You may want to practice with Story View. Now that your file has been saved, just be sure not to save it again, simply close the file and do not save the changes when you're done.

Storyline assumes your course content will flow in linear fashion, from one slide to the next, as shown by the arrows between slides. Storyline automatically numbers slides and scenes sequentially. If you want the **Home** slide to come after the **Menu** slide, all you need to do is to click on the **Menu** slide and drag it up. A blue arrow will appear indicating where the slide will be placed. Once you release the mouse, you'll notice that the slides are automatically renumbered to reflect the move.

You can manipulate the view in Story View by clicking on the small minus icons to collapse and plus icons to expand scenes and using the zoom controls in the lower-right corner.

Summary

This chapter covered the basic formatting tasks and expanded our course with new slides and scenes. If you have used PowerPoint in the past, you may have noticed how similar Storyline is; a lot of its basic features work just like they do in Microsoft Office.

It's always good practice to save your work often. With Storyline you can also preview your work frequently to make sure that animations, object placement, and formatting styles look and behave the way you expect. The **Preview** function in Storyline is speedy and it's an amazing timesaver; checking as you go makes for fewer changes at the end.

You're already discovering how much you can do in Storyline without being a designer or developer. It takes a lot less effort to make an e-learning course look good and even less to make it interactive. Just remember to keep your work simple and focus on how to use the tool to best educate those who will be taking your courses. In the next chapter we'll explore how to add interactivity to a story.

3
Adding Interactivity

Storyline has two powerful features at the core of its authoring environment: *states* and *triggers*. States can change the way an object appears and triggers can add action to your story. The combination of these two features creates an endless variety of interactions.

Interactivity is really all about *action*. Rarely is something interactive without a resulting action. An example would be clicking or touching a button that displays the next slide. In Storyline, the button is the *object*, the click/touch of the button is the *event* and moving to the next slide is the action. But action can also occur based on a condition rather than user input. For example, a slide (object) can automatically advance to the next slide (action) when the timeline ends (event).

States change the appearance of an object. For example, when a button is clicked or touched, it changes color from green to red. The change of color is a change of state from the default green (*normal*) to red (*selected*). State changes occur based on some kind of action: whether caused by user input or by a condition.

This chapter covers the basics of adding action to a story; both user interaction and conditional actions in addition to controlling object appearance and behavior.

In this chapter you will learn:

- More about states and triggers
- How to add hyperlinks and buttons to a slide's content
- Additional formatting tips to add finesse to your example story
- How to quickly publish to validate functionality

Follow along...

The exercise at the end of *Chapter 2, Adding Content into your Story*, created a file called `Exercise 2 - Workplace Compliance`. This file should be open in Storyline before continuing.

Working with states

States alter the appearance of objects and are a great way of providing visual cues and feedback to learners. You could use states to:

- Indicate course progress when a topic is complete
- Add a glow to a button or image when hovered over
- Pop up a definition when the mouse rolls over a word

States can be applied to any object on a slide including images, shapes, text boxes, and captions. By default, an object has just one state called normal and this is what you see before any event happens that may trigger a change of state to the object.

There are eight built-in states. Built-in states are triggered automatically and don't require additional setup for them to function. For example, the state called hover will automatically be triggered when the user hovers the mouse over an object that has a hover state assigned to it.

You can also create your own custom states. Custom states are given a unique name by you and are triggered manually. Custom states are often used when user input, such as a mouse click, isn't needed. Usually a condition of some form triggers the state change.

You can change the appearance of any state using all the standard formatting commands including font, color, effects, size, alignment, and so on. Not only can each state have different formatting, but each state can also have additional objects associated with it, including sounds and animations.

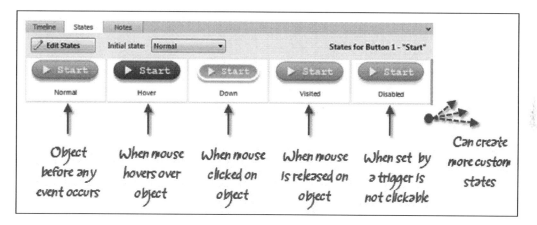

To create and manage states, you will need to use the **States** tab located in the **Timeline**, **States**, and **Notes** panel as shown in the screen shots here.

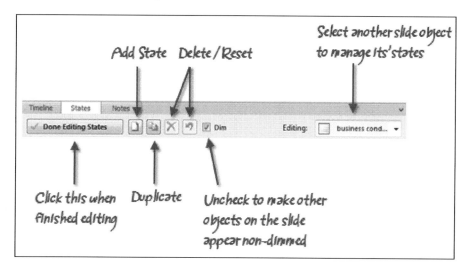

Here's how to create a state:

1. Click on the object to which you would like to add a state.
2. Click on the **States** tab.
3. Click on **Edit States** and then click on the **New State** icon that appears to the right of the **Done Editing States** button.
4. Select a new state using any of the built-in state names as displayed in the drop-down list, or type a new state name.
5. Click on **Add**. The new state appears in the list of available states for the object that you selected.
6. To create another new state, you can click on **Add** again or select one of the existing available states by clicking on the state (a yellow highlight will appear around the selected state). Click on the **Duplicate** icon to create a copy with the same formatting.
7. When finished editing, click on the **Done Editing States** button to save your changes.

 By default, other objects on the slide dim when you're creating or editing states. You can uncheck the **Dim** checkbox from the **States** panel to display all objects on the slide normally.

Here's how to edit a state:

1. Click on the object that you would like to add a state to.
2. Click on the **States** tab.
3. Click on **Edit States**. At this point, you can select any of the states listed and perform the following tasks:
   - Delete the state by clicking on the **Delete** icon.
   - Reset the state back to the normal state by clicking on the **Reset** icon.
   - Use any of the standard object formatting features to adjust the look and feel of the object. For example, you can add a glow to an object's hover state by clicking on the **Format** tab, selecting **Shape Effects**, and applying a glow to the object. The glow effect will only be displayed when the user hovers the mouse over the object.
4. After you finish editing, click on the **Done Editing States** button to save your changes.

To save time, you can use the **Editing states on** the drop-down list on the right side of the **States** panel to edit objects that are on the same slide. When you scroll over items in the list, an outline is displayed to highlight the currently selected object. Make any changes necessary to the object. Changes to all objects are saved when you click on the **Done Editing States** button.

You can use **Format Painter** on the **Home** tab to quickly apply the formatting of the selected object, including its states, to another.

By default, the initial state is always **Normal**, but when an object has more than one state, you can specify an initial state other than **Normal**. You can even specify **Hidden** as the initial state, which means the object won't appear until triggered.

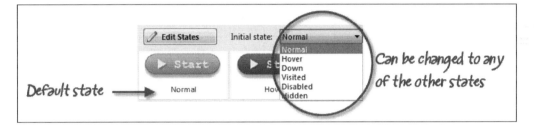

Working with triggers

Triggers are used whenever you need to create action. Triggers can be used to do things such as:

- Jump from slide to slide
- Open a web page
- Submit a quiz
- Play a sound or video clip

Triggers are displayed in the **Triggers** panel and organized into three groups: *slide triggers* (timeline start or end), *object triggers* (state or interaction with an object), and *player triggers* (player buttons next, back, and submit).

The order of triggers is very important since triggers are processed sequentially in order of appearance from top to bottom. Having triggers in the wrong order will produce unexpected results. For example, if you want to change the state of an image before advancing to the next slide, the image state trigger must appear before the slide advance trigger in the **Triggers** panel.

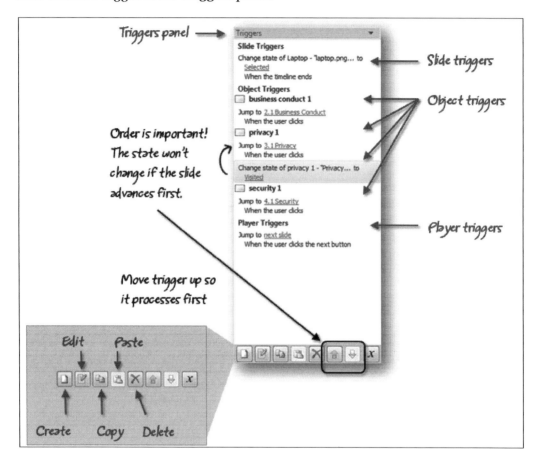

Triggers can be applied to any type of object and are activated by an event of some form. There are 14 different types of events that can activate a trigger, which can be seen on the left-hand side of the following screenshot.

Once activated, there are 21 different kinds of actions that can result; those are listed on the right-hand side of the following screenshot:

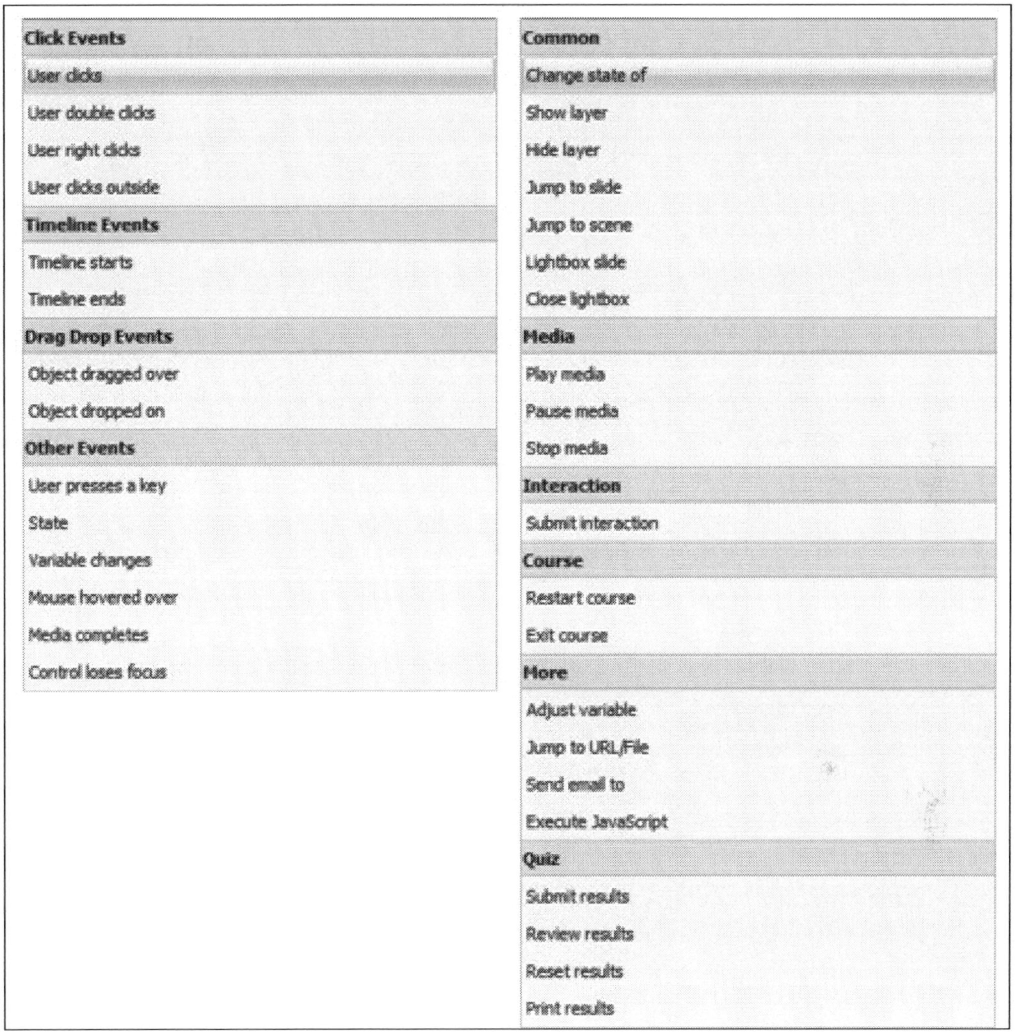

Click Events	Common
User clicks	Change state of
User double clicks	Show layer
User right clicks	Hide layer
User clicks outside	Jump to slide
Timeline Events	Jump to scene
Timeline starts	Lightbox slide
Timeline ends	Close lightbox
Drag Drop Events	**Media**
Object dragged over	Play media
Object dropped on	Pause media
Other Events	Stop media
User presses a key	**Interaction**
State	Submit interaction
Variable changes	**Course**
Mouse hovered over	Restart course
Media completes	Exit course
Control loses focus	**More**
	Adjust variable
	Jump to URL/File
	Send email to
	Execute JavaScript
	Quiz
	Submit results
	Review results
	Reset results
	Print results

To create a trigger, perform the following steps:

1. Click on the **Create new trigger** icon in the **Triggers** panel or click on the **Insert** tab and choose **Interactive Objects** and then **Trigger**.

2. When the **Trigger Wizard** window appears, perform the following steps:

   1. Choose what action should result from the **Action** drop-down.

   2. Select where this action should happen from the drop-down menu that appears below **Action** (refer to the following screenshot). The name of this drop down will change depending on which action has been selected. For example, **Slide** appears if **Jump to Slide** is the action selected.

   3. Select when the action occurs in the **When** drop-down.

   4. You should also confirm with which object the trigger is associated in the **Object** drop down. This will default to the currently selected object, but you can change this if needed.

   5. Click on **OK**.

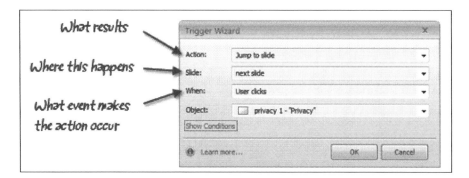

3. You should preview the project to test the functionality of the new trigger.

 The options in the **Action** drop-down menu stay the same, while the options within **Slide**, **When**, and **Object** change depending on the action that is selected.

Perform the following steps to change the order of triggers:

1. In the **Triggers** panel, click on the trigger you would like to move.
2. Click on the up or down arrow at the bottom of the **Triggers** panel to reposition it.

Perform the following steps to copy, paste, duplicate, and delete triggers:

1. In the **Triggers** panel, click on the trigger you wish to copy, paste, duplicate, or delete.
2. Click on the appropriate icon at the bottom of the **Triggers** panel to perform the action. You can also use the following shortcut keys instead:

    ○   *Ctrl + C* to copy
    ○   *Ctrl + V* to paste
    ○   *Delete* to delete

 You may find it faster to copy and paste existing triggers to new objects rather than creating triggers from scratch each time you need one. To do this, copy a trigger and then paste it onto one or more objects by clicking on a single object or while pressing *Ctrl* or *Shift* and clicking on multiple objects. Press *Ctrl + V* to paste the trigger to the object(s). After pasting the trigger, you can select the trigger in the **Triggers** panel to quickly make any adjustment to it. Note that when you duplicate a slide object, the triggers on that object are also copied.

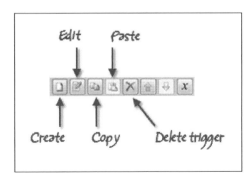

Follow along...

Using Exercise 2 - Workplace Compliance, you'll add states to objects, quickly replicate formatting and triggers to multiple objects, and create navigation consistency with master slides.

1. Double-click to view the **1.2 Menu** slide and select the Business Conduct note.

2. Click on the **States** tab and then choose **Edit States**.

3. Add a new state using the pre-built state named **Hover**.

4. Duplicate this new state using the pre-built state named **Visited**.

5. Select the **Hover** state and perform the following steps:

    1. Resize the note to be larger by dragging the bottom-left corner.

    2. Change the font color to red.

    3. Click on the **Visited** state and, from the **Insert** tab, add a checkmark to the upper-right side of the note. Fill the note with green color and add a shadow.

    4. Click on **Done Editing States**.

6. While still selecting the **Business Conduct** note, click on the **Create new trigger** icon and define the action to jump to slide, choose the slide **2.1 Business Conduct**, and click on **OK**.

7. With the **Business Conduct** note still selected, click on **Format Painter** from the **Home** tab and click on the **Privacy** note. Repeat this for the **Security** note.

8. Click on the trigger for the **Business Conduct** note in the **Triggers** panel and press *Ctrl + C* to copy the trigger. On the slide, select both the *Privacy* and *Security* notes, and press *Ctrl + V* to paste the trigger onto them.

9. Edit the **Privacy** and **Security** note triggers so that they jump to the slides **3.1 Privacy** and **4.1 Security** respectively.

10. From the **Animations** tab, set **Slide Transition** to **Uncover Down**.

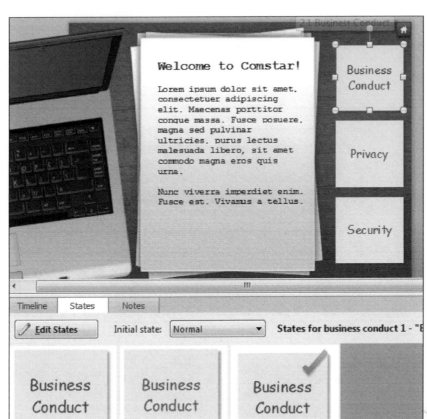

11. Preview this scene and check to make sure the home button works and the hover effects work on the post-it notes.

12. Save the file under a new name, Exercise 3 - Workplace Compliance.

Adding hyperlinks

Storyline uses triggers to create hyperlinks. By default, you can hyperlink to a web location (URL) or a document (local), but since hyperlinks are triggers, you can also choose another action such as jumping to a slide.

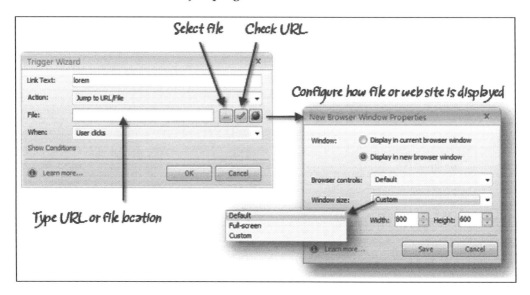

Perform the following steps to insert a hyperlink:

1. Select the item to which you want to add a hyperlink. If this is text, click-and-drag to select just the portion of text where you would like the hyperlink to appear.

2. Press *Ctrl + K*, right-click, and choose **Hyperlink** or click on the **Insert** tab and choose **Hyperlink**.

3. The **Trigger Wizard** window appears, with the options discussed in the following steps displayed:

   1. **Link text** is the text that is linked. You can change the wording of the link text, if you wish.

   2. Select what action should be taken when the user clicks on the object. This defaults to **Jump to URL/File**.

   3. Enter a filename or select a file by clicking on the **File** icon or typing a web address (URL). You can click on the **Check URL** button to make sure the web address is valid.

   4. Click on the **Configure** icon to determine how the window containing the file or URL will be displayed and what size it should be. Click on **Save** and then **OK**.

You can format the color of a text hyperlink by working with the design theme for the course in a way similar to PowerPoint. Here's how:

1. Choose the **Design** tab and click on the **Colors** drop-down menu.

2. If the project is using a default color theme and you don't want to alter the original theme, select **Create New Theme Colors**.

3. If the project is using a custom color theme and you want to edit that theme, right-click on the theme and choose **Edit**.

4. Locate the **Hyperlink** color in the theme color list and change it.

5. If creating a new theme, you can give it a name, otherwise click on **Save**.

Adding buttons

Buttons are an easy way of adding interactivity to a course. Storyline comes with rectangular and oval buttons pre-configured with 6 states (normal, hover, down, visited, and disabled). You can customize these states and add your own.

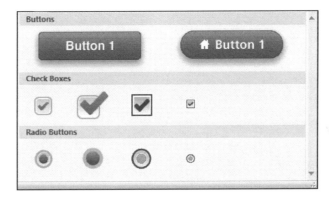

Buttons can be formatted using quick styles that are part of the current theme found under the **Format** tab. They can be resized and moved just as you would for other objects.

Holding down the *Shift* key while dragging any handle of a shape constrains the aspect ratio while resizing it. Holding down the *Shift* key while drawing a new rectangle or oval shape will constrain your shape to a perfect square or circle.

Button icons

Storyline provides a library of over 100 icons that can be added to any button, either with or without text. The color of the icon can be set from the **Format** tab and the size of the icon can be adjusted by changing the font size under the **Home** tab.

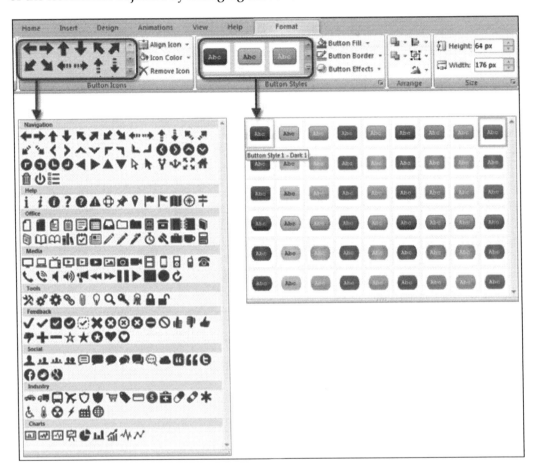

 If you customize the look of a button and want to re-use this formatting for new buttons in the course, you can do this by right-clicking on the button and choosing **Set As Default**. Once you do this, new buttons created in the same story will take on this default button format.

Perform the following steps to insert a button:

1. Select the **Insert** tab and then choose **Button**.
2. Pick a button style.
3. Click-and-drag on the slide to position and size the button.

Perform the following steps to format a button:

1. Select the button.
2. Begin typing, if you wish to add text.
3. Select the **Format** tab and choose from any of the formatting options.
4. Add an icon to the button by selecting an icon style and color.

Follow along...

In this exercise, you will continue to work with the file, Exercise 3 - Workplace Compliance, to add interactivity, external content, and animated effects.

1. View the **Master Slide** and select **Master Slide Layout 2**.
2. Insert a small button in the upper-right corner of the slide. Include a house icon on this button and change the color to grey.
3. In the **Triggers** panel, click on the **Add a trigger** link on the new button and configure the action so that it jumps to the slide **1.2 Menu** when clicked.

4. Return to Normal View and navigate to **1.1 Home**. Add a new rectangle button placed over the top of the words **Compliance Matters!** on the slide.

5. Rename the button in the timeline from **Button 1** to start.

6. Format the new button so that it has a green fill, the word **Start** on it, and a right arrow icon to the left of the word **Start**.

7. Change the **Hover** state of the start button to a grey fill.

8. In the **Triggers** panel, change the trigger for the **Start** button so that it jumps to the next slide (**1.2 Menu**) when the user clicks on it.

9. Slide the **Start** button to the 3.5 second mark in the timeline. This will force the button to display only after the **Compliance Matters!** tagline appears.

10. Expand the **Sub-title** group in the timeline and add a fade out animation to compliance matters and a fade in and fade out animation to compliance box.

11. Expand the employee group in the timeline, click on the employee object, click on the **States** panel, and add a new state called **Happy** from the pre-built states.

12. Add a slide trigger that manipulates the employee image when the slide ends. Do this by selecting the employee object (not the employee group, rather the single employee object within the employee group), click on **Add new trigger** in the **Triggers** panel and set the trigger to change the state of the employee object to **Happy** when the timeline of slide **1.1 Home** ends.

13. Save the file.

14. Navigate to **1.4 Privacy**. Be sure that you are in Normal View.

15. You'll now link the Google search result image that you captured in an earlier lesson so that it links to a live website. To do this, open your browser, go to Google, and search for the definition of corporate privacy. When the search results appear, select the URL from the browser address bar and press *Ctrl + C* to copy it.

16. Back on the **1.4 Privacy** slide, select the Google image and choose **Format | Hyperlink**. In the **Action** drop down, select **Jump to URL/File** and then press *Ctrl + V* to paste the URL into the **File** field.

17. Select the **Browser options** icon to the right of the **File** field (it's a globe) and set it so that there are no browser controls and the size of the pop-up window is custom at 800 px x 600 px. Click on **OK** to save those changes.

18. You may need to move the Google image or resize it so that it doesn't overlap the **Home** button you earlier added to the Master Slide.

19. Preview this slide and save the file. You will notice that the web link is not active during preview and the earlier zoom placed on the Google image is not that necessary. Let's remove it by closing out of **Preview**, selecting the Google image, and choosing **Format | Zoom**.

20. Save the file.

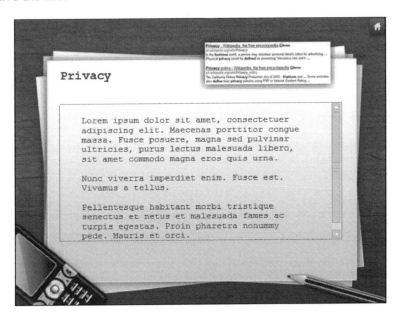

Quick publishing

Preview helps catch functionality and formatting errors. It is your main tool for quickly testing as you develop. But it's also a good practice to publish a working sample of your project every now and again. Publishing generates a full working sample and includes features such as links, web objects, videos, and engages interactions that can't be seen when previewing. Publishing also lets you test your project in multiple browsers and on multiple monitors to catch formatting and display issues.

Publishing is straightforward and relatively quick even on larger projects. For testing purposes, using the option **Publish to the web** works best for quick checks.

 If you are designing a course for deployment on mobile devices, there are other considerations to keep in mind, namely the differences between Flash, HTML5, and iOS outputs (refer to the *Appendix*). More details on the publishing process will be covered in *Chapter 10, Publishing your Story*

Perform the following steps to publish to the web:

1. Choose **Publish** from the **Home** tab.
2. Select **Web**, the topmost publishing option that is listed.
3. Storyline takes the title from the name of your file; you can change this when publishing is to be more or less descriptive, but avoid using special characters and spaces. The title appears by default in the upper-left corner of the course interface and can be turned on or off.
4. Choose a folder in which to place the published output by typing a path or clicking on the ellipses icon and navigating to a location.
5. Click on **Publish**.
6. Click on **View Project**.

A note on viewing with different browsers:

When you click **View Project** upon completion of publishing, Storyline will open the published project in your default web browser. It's a good practice to test the published output in different browsers and on different monitors throughout the development process. This helps catch cross-browser functionality and design issues.

 Storyline publishes into a folder given the same name as the title, followed by the word output, for example, `Workplace Compliance output`. Inside the published folder, there is a file titled `story.html`. This can be double-clicked to launch the course, or you can right-click, choose **Open with** and select a browser other than your default browser to view the published output.

Follow along...

In this final exercise, you'll use the file `Exercise 3 - Workplace Compliance` to add zooming to images along with minor formatting tasks. At the end of this exercise, you will publish your work.

1. Navigate to the **1.2 Business Conduct** slide and be sure that you are in Normal View.

2. There are Polaroid images that come with the template. You can customize these by swapping out the images with something more specific to your course. To do this, click on the image three times. This will select the inner image that appears inside the Polaroid. You can also expand the picture group in the timeline and select the image this way.

3. Once the image is selected, right-click and choose **Change Picture...**, and then navigate to where an appropriate image is on your local computer or network. Click on **Open** to swap the image out with a new one.

4. Since the Polaroids are quite small, let's add a zoom on the inner picture by selecting it and choosing **Format | Zoom**. You can repeat these steps, if you wish, for the second Polaroid.

5. Reduce the size of the calculator image, space out the Polaroids, and add a little rotation. You are aiming for a bit of "white space" and balance.

6. Preview this slide and check out the zooms you've inserted. When done, close **Preview** and save the project.

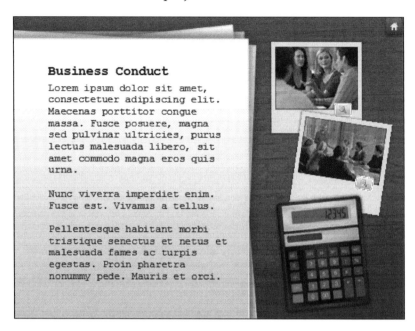

7. Now it's time to publish and test the entire course from start to finish. To do this, click on the **Publish** button from the **Home** tab, select **Web**, change the title to **Compliance Matters**, and select a location where you would like to store the published output. Click on **Publish** to start the process.

8. When publishing is finished, you can choose the **View Project** button to test your course or you can navigate to the published output folder and double-click on `story.html` to launch the course in your default browser or **right-click**, choose Open with and select other browsers.

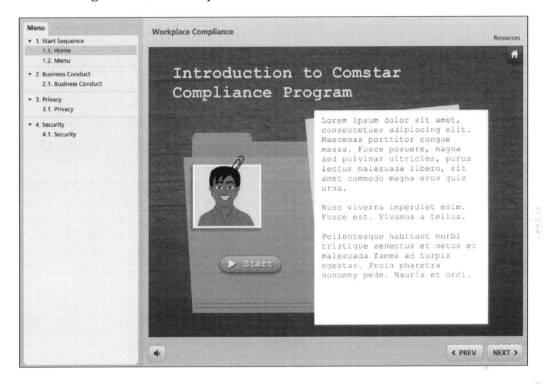

Summary

This chapter introduced two very powerful features of Storyline: states and triggers, to help you create content that is dynamic, intelligent, and responsive to the learner.

The power of the *no programming zone* should be evident by now. Ease of use and the ability to customize objects, states, and triggers creates huge potential for creating exactly the kind of content and interaction you hoped you could: without a team of 10!

In the previous chapter, **Preview** was used as a method of reviewing the work you are developing. You will rely on **Preview** often, but it's also a good practice to publish every now and again, particularly after adding a series of new slides or new interactions. Double-checking that your work functions correctly in different browsers and looks the way you expect on different monitors throughout development will save you time later in the development cycle, and goes a long way to ensuring the course operates properly for your intended audience.

Now that you have an understanding of adding interactivity to a story, let's focus on features and techniques to make a course more approachable and engaging for your audience. For this we need to add a human touch. We will learn how to do this, in the next chapter.

4

Adding Characters and Audio

The most effective and engaging e-learning courses are ones that feel real. These courses seem to reach out and touch the learner in a way that motivates them to happily continue. This kind of connection is gold; it is the moment when real learning happens, the kind of learning that is understood and retained long after the course ends.

This chapter focuses on using Storyline features that can help you create a human touch to your courses. Specifically, you'll learn the following:

- How to add photographic and illustrated characters into an e-learning course
- What expressions and poses are available
- Techniques to adjust character size and position
- How to create interactive conversations using characters
- How to add and edit narration, both audio and captions

Examples of the human touch done well

Before diving into specific Storyline features, let's examine examples of e-learning that have a human touch and discover why this works so well for almost any subject matter. Each example mentioned here is accompanied by a URL; take a moment to review each example before continuing with this chapter:

- *Connect with Haji Kamal* by *Cathy Moore*: A lieutenant needs to make a good impression on a tribal leader in Afghanistan and you can help him (http://blog.cathy-moore.com/2010/05/elearning-example-branching-scenario/)
- *Mi Vida Loca* by BBC: Learn Spanish while a mystery unfolds (http://www.bbc.co.uk/languages/spanish/mividaloca/)

- *Mouse Party* by University of Utah: Learn how drugs alter the brains of mice (`http://learn.genetics.utah.edu/content/addiction/drugs/mouse.html`)

- *Homestand* by Roanoke Time: A look behind the scenes at a baseball game (http://www.roanoke.com/sports/homestand/multimedia/interactive.html)

- Noble Prize winner *Blood typing game*. Figure out each patient's blood type and give them a transfusion before it's too late (`http://www.nobelprize.org/educational/medicine/bloodtypinggame/game/index.html`)

- *Make the Sale* by Suddenly Smart: Finding the right solution for a customer (`http://www.suddenlysmart.com/examples/global_ex1/player.html`)

- *Using Computer Ports* by Suddenly Smart: Help a colleague quickly set up a laptop for an important presentation (`http://www.suddenlysmart.com/examples/computerports2/player.html`)

Each of these examples has a common thread; though they cover different topics, all do so using a human touch. This isn't about specific graphics, audio, video, animations, or interactivity. Rather, it's about understanding the subject matter and knowing how to reframe for the learner. The most direct route is to rewrite content from a telling approach to a what's-in-it-for-me approach. This helps focus on the learner and helps them understand as opposed to information delivery only.

Here are some additional tips on how you can create a connection with the learner:

- **Create a likeness of self**: The *Homestand* example is simple but effective because of the way video is used. The learner can see a mini-human just like them in action and the learner is at the controls. This is interesting and empowering and it instantly creates a connection. The learner wants to click and make the person do different things. The Result is learning without any effort at all. A nice place to be.

- **Create realistic situations**: The *Connect with Haji Kamal* and BBC's *Mi Vida Loca* are two great examples of connecting with the learner, bringing the learner directly into the story. It is compelling because it's contextual, realistic, and unfolds based on the learner's choice. From a media perspective, the characters don't have to be high quality video or images; sketched illustrations work equally well because the content is so well designed.

- **Allow participation and choice**: All of the examples provide a choice and allow the learner to make complex, not complicated, decisions. The *Mouse Party* example simulates your arm going into a mouse tank, which provides an interesting level of reality as does the *Blood typing game*, particularly if you make a mistake.

- **Keep it concise and focused**: The examples mentioned earlier have this in common. None of them preface the learning with lengthy explanations or instructions. The content is framed with the learner in mind. Appropriate, contextual feedback is offered. This approach helps bring the learner into the story, helps them pay attention, and helps maintain interest in the subject matter.

About Storyline characters

Storyline provides built-in characters that you can add to a slide. The Characters feature is very useful if you don't have access to a wide range of stock photography and if you want to use more than just a single pose or expression.

There are several illustrated built-in male and female characters and they come in a variety of different hairstyles, clothing, poses, and expressions. Also included is one complete photographic female character.

Characters can be inserted as static images or can be made dynamic and interactive using states and triggers, the latter providing you with the ability to create responsive conversations for the learner. Once inserted, you can modify the character as you would modify any other image; moving, resizing, cropping, animating, or applying image effects such as glows and shadows.

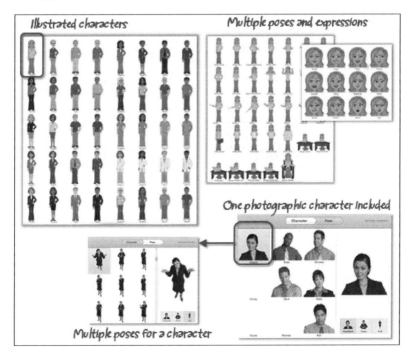

Character states

You can add states to a character to show different expressions or poses. The different views of a character can be displayed based on a trigger, timeline event, or user action.

For example, you could insert a character that provides an instruction to begin a quiz. If the learner makes a mistake during the quiz, the same character with a different pose appears with feedback. When they finish, another pose appears congratulating the learner.

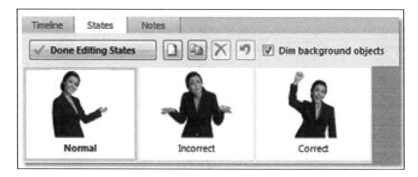

The example uses custom states. These states were specifically created to show the incorrect and correct poses that are triggered to display after the user submits a quiz.

Of course you can always use the built-in states, if it makes sense to do so. One example is to use a hover state so, if the learner rolls the mouse over the character, the character responds by changing pose and providing a hint.

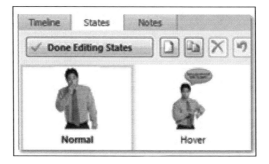

Adding a character

Characters can be inserted into your project from the **Insert** tab in the ribbon, whereas adding or changing the state of a character is done using the **Timeline**, **States**, and **Notes** panel. Let's take a look at the steps to do this:

1. While in the **Normal** view, select the **Insert** tab and click on **Character** in the **Illustrations** section of the ribbon.

2. Choose the **Illustrated** or **Photographic** character.

3. Select the character to insert by scrolling through the available options on the left side of the **Characters** dialog box. Click to select the character and it will appear on the right side of the screen.

4. For now, pick a stance for the normal state and later on you can add other states as needed. Choose from the options that are below the selected character on the right side of the screen. For illustrated characters, this will be left, center, or right. For photographic characters, this will be headshot, torso, or full. If working with an illustrated character, you can select **Expression** from the top of the screen and select one of several facial expressions.

5. Pick a pose by clicking on the **Pose** option at the top of the screen.

6. Click on **Insert** when done.

Adding a state to a character

Follow these steps to add a state to the character:

1. Select the character on the slide that you want to add a new state to.

2. Click on the **States** tab and then click on **Edit States**.

3. Click on the **New State** button.

4. When prompted for a state name, select either one of the built-in states, or insert a new state's name to use a custom state.

Follow along...

The exercise at the end of *Chapter 3, Adding Interactivity,* created a file called `Exercise 3 - Workplace Compliance`. This file should be open in Storyline before continuing. In this exercise, you will add a new global button to trigger the display of a character who asks the learner if they need help.

1. In the `Exercise 3 - Workplace Compliance` file, navigate to the **Menu** slide and switch to the **Normal** view.

2. Insert a button in the lower-right corner, similar in size to the **Home** button that appears in the upper-right corner. Change the color to blue and add a question mark icon.

3. Edit the hover state of the button so that you can insert a help character. Follow these steps:

    1. Click on the question mark icon on the slide, select the **States** panel and click on **Edit States**.

    2. Select the **Hover** state.

    3. Select the **Insert** tab, choose **Character**, and select the **Photographic** character.

    4. Atsumi is the default female character, select this character from the left side of the **Characters** screen and then select **Torso** from the lower-right corner.

    5. Select **Pose** from the top of the **Characters** screen and choose a pose that gestures to the left.

    6. Click on **Insert**.

    7. Position the character to the left of the question mark button and enlarge the size of the character until her hand is touching the word **Privacy** on the yellow post-it note.

    8. Select the character and choose **Format | Rotate | Flip Horizontal** from the ribbon.

    9. Move the character around until the image is aligned with the bottom of the slide and appears to the left of the question mark button.

4. While still editing the hover state, let's add a textbox to display help information:

    1. Insert a rectangle in the center of the slide making it about 300 px x 400 px in size.

    2. Make the outline black and the fill black with a 10 percent transparency.

    3. Add an outer shadow of **Offset Diagonal Bottom Right**.

    4. Insert the text, as shown at the end of this exercise, into the rectangle.

    5. Format the text to *Arial 16pt Bold* for the first line and *Arial 14pt* for the remaining. Be sure to add bullets for the paragraphs that are below the first line and left align all text.

    6. Position the rectangle so that it appears to be touching the characters.

5. Next, let's animate these two objects:

    1. Click on the character, choose the **Animations** tab, and add an **Entrance** animation of **Fly In** from the **Bottom** section.

    2. Click on the textbox and add an **Entrance** animation of **Fly In** from the **Left** section.

6. Click on **Done Editing States**.

7. Press *CTRL + F12* to preview just this slide. Test the new help button.

8. If everything is working correctly, exit preview and save the file under a new name, Exercise 4 - Workplace Compliance.

About character conversations

Character conversations are often used to mimic real-life interactions. Most frequently you will see character conversations in scenarios or as a method to test learner understanding of a particular concept. The following example shows how a character can prompt the learner to make a choice and another character respond to that choice.

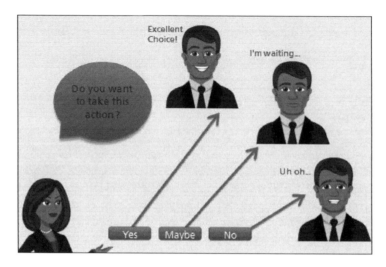

Speech bubbles

The Captions feature provides additional shapes that are designed to be used as captions, pop ups, or alerts, and also as visual instructions or conversations in speech bubbles.

Captions can be placed, sized, and formatted the same way you would format a regular shape or image in Storyline.

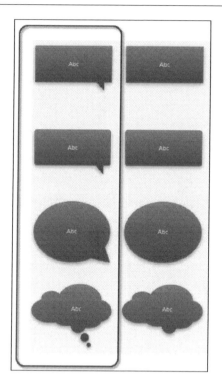

Adding a speech bubble

Speech bubbles are found in the **Captions** menu in Storyline. Follow these steps:

1. Select the **Insert** tab and choose **Captions**.
2. Select a speech bubble style from the left side of the **Captions** styles.
3. Draw the shape onto the slide.
4. Drag the yellow handle on the point of the speech bubble to change its position and shape.

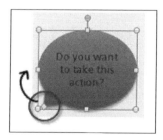

5. Add text and format as you normally would.

Audible conversation

Adding a human voice to the conversation can be an effective method of making a connection with the learner. You can record narration directly within Storyline or use an external software application to do this and then import the audio clip into Storyline.

 It is recommended to use the selected method consistently throughout the project to maintain sound levels and quality across slides.

Storyline supports a variety of audio formats including `.aac`, `.aiff`, `.aif`, `.m4a`, `.ogg`, `.wmv`, `.wav`, and `.mp3`. When you record narration, `.mp3` files are generated with an audio bitrate of 192 kbps (kilobits per second). The quality of the audio clips in a story can be adjusted prior to publishing.

Recording narration

When you record or import narration, it will appear in the Timeline wherever the Playhead is currently positioned. You can position the Playhead to the appropriate place in the Timeline before recording, or after dragging the resulting audio clip left or right in the Timeline.

 You will likely rely on some kind of script to read narration from. Often the narration script is provided to learners in the form of slide notes that provide a written transcript of spoken narration. This transcript is not true Closed Captions that follow along as narration plays; rather, the entire script is presented at once. Placing the script in the **Notes** panel of a slide makes the script available to the learner with the exception of when a slide is viewed in a lightbox; in this case, the Notes feature is not accessible. When recording, you can use the slide notes to read scripted narration.

You can record narration using the **Insert** tab and then selecting **Sound**. You will see the **Record Microphone** window appear with various controls to record and edit your narration.

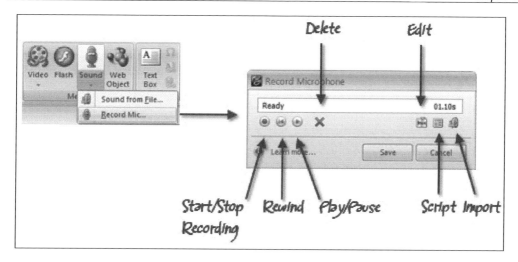

To record a narration, follow these steps:

1. Select the **Insert** tab and click on the **Sound** button.

2. Select **Record Mic**.

3. Click on the **Record** button and speak into your microphone.

4. Click on the **Stop** button when you have finished recording.

5. You may want to click on the **Play** button to listen to the recording, click on **Record** if you wish to re-record the narration or on **Delete** to remove the entire audio clip from the slide.

6. Click on the **Save** button to save the recording.

 After recording or importing, a speaker icon appears in the lower-left corner of the slide area indicating audio is present on the slide. You can double-click on this icon to play the clip.

Importing an audio clip

You can also import existing narration from the same menu, using the following steps:

1. Select the **Insert** tab and click on the **Sound** button.

2. Select **Sound** from **File** and find the file you want to import.

3. Click on the **Open** button to import the file.

When you import slides from PowerPoint, Articulate Quizmaker, or other Storyline projects, all audio files associated with the external content will be available for editing. The exception is Articulate Engage where the audio is imported but cannot be edited within Storyline as it is part of a Flash-based interaction. Note also that because Engage interactions are Flash, they cannot be played back on mobile devices.

Editing an audio track

Storyline provides a built-in audio editor that allows you to perform basic editing tasks on a recorded or imported audio clip.

From the editor, you will see a **waveform** of your narration and from here you can playback the clip, adjust volume, delete portions, and insert a silent track (this is handy when you need to space out the narration or create a pause).

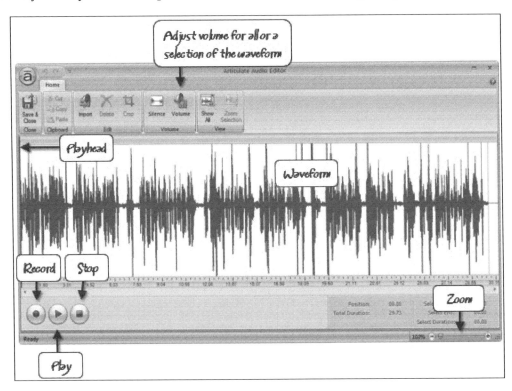

Here are the steps for editing audio:

1. Double-click on the audio clip in the Timeline to open the **Audio Editor**.

2. If editing or playing back just a portion of the clip, select it first by clicking on it and dragging it on the waveform to highlight a portion of the clip.

3. Perform the required editing tasks including re-recording, if needed.

4. You can cut- or copy-and-paste audio by selecting the section to cut or copy, clicking on the **Cut** (*Ctrl* + *X*) or **Copy** (*Ctrl* + *C*) buttons from the ribbon and then selecting where you want to paste the audio in the waveform and pressing *Ctrl* + *V* to paste.

Accessing sound tools

Once the audio has been inserted, you can access Storyline features that deal specifically with audio in a few different ways:

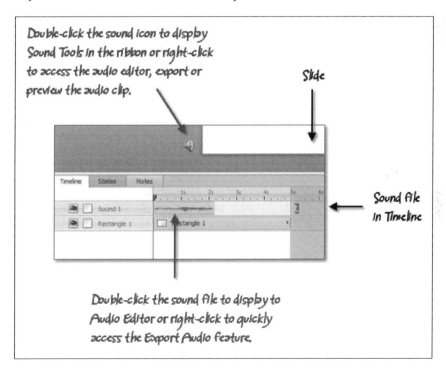

Synchronizing objects and narration

You'll likely want to synchronize slide objects to your narration, particularly when a slide plays back automatically without learner interaction. You can use **cue points** in Storyline to make objects appear at the right moment.

Cue points can be inserted in the Timeline by listening to the narration and inserting a cue point where you want a slide object to appear. Once you've added your cue points, you can then align individual slide objects to them. You cannot align a group of objects to a cue point without first expanding the group and then individually aligning the objects within the group.

You can manually insert a cue point by right-clicking on the Timeline and choosing **Insert Cue Point at Playhead**. You can insert as many cue points as you need, each will appear in the Timeline and are sequentially numbered.

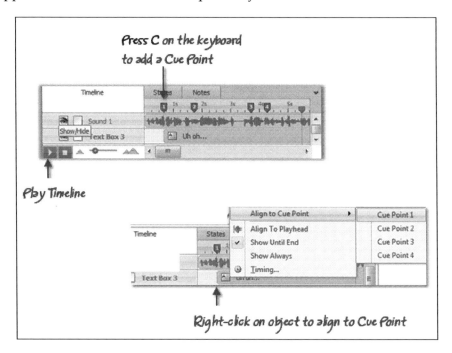

 Cue points aren't necessary when synchronization isn't needed (for example, audio plays automatically when the learner interacts with an object) or if there are few slide objects and minimal narration (you can easily manually adjust objects to start at a specific point in the Timeline).

Adding cue points

Here's how to do this:

1. Click on the **Play** button in the lower-right corner of the Timeline to begin slide playback (animation and audio).

2. Press *C* on the keyboard when you want to insert a cue point. If you wish to manually adjust it further, click-and-drag the cue point marker to the left or right in the Timeline.

3. Once done, right-click on an object in the Timeline and choose **Align to Cue Point**. Then, select the cue point number to align the object to that cue point.

4. If you no longer need a cue point, right-click on the cue point in the Timeline and choose **Delete Cue Point**.

Follow along...

Continuing with Exercise 4 - Workplace Compliance, you will now create an audio narration to add a human touch to the start of this course and for the help character.

1. For this exercise, you will use the audio recording capabilities in Storyline to record the welcome information. Navigate to the **Menu** slide and select the **Notes** panel.

2. Type the following narration script in the **Notes** panel:

   Hello and welcome to this course. There are three topics to cover: Business Conduct, Privacy, and Security. You can explore these topics in any order you wish.

3. Let's record it. Select **Insert | Sound | Record Mic...**.

4. Click on the **Narration Script** icon to display the script.

5. When ready, click on the **Record** icon (it displays a red circle) to begin. There will be a 3-second countdown before recording starts. Record the script as shown.

6. When done, click on the **Record** icon again (it now displays a square) to stop the recording.

7. Click on the **Play** button to listen to the recording.

8. If everything sounds good, click on the **Save** button, otherwise you can replay, rerecord, or edit the audio first.

9. A **Sound** icon appears off the lower-left corner of the slide confirming the sound was recorded and is now part of the slide. Switch to the Timeline to see the waveform representation of the sound. This displays at the top of the Timeline and is called **Sound 1**.

10. Let's time the three post-it notes so that they appear on screen as the narrator speaks of each. Follow these steps:

    1. Click on the **Play** button in the lower-left corner of the Timeline. The audio will begin playing.

    2. Press the *C* button on the keyboard when you hear "Business Conduct".

    3. Repeat this for "Privacy" and "Security".

    4. Right-click on the **Business Conduct** object in the Timeline, choose **Align to Cue Point** and select **Cue Point 1**.

    5. Repeat for the other post-it notes aligning to **Cue Point 2** and **Cue Point 3**.

11. Press *Ctrl + F12* to preview this slide. Close **Preview** and make any adjustments necessary to ensure each post-it appears at the proper time. You can do this by dragging the cue point markers right or left and re-aligning the objects to them.

12. Let's add a voice to our help character. Select the question mark button, click on the **States** panel and select **Edit States**.

13. Click on the **Hover** state.

14. Not sure what each topic is about? Here's a quick explanation:

    1. Select **Insert | Sound | Record Mic...** and record the following narration:

2. Play and edit the recording if needed. Save when done. You will notice a **Sound** icon appearing next to the question mark button. This audio, as part of a state, will play automatically when the state is activated.

3. Click on **Done Editing States**.

4. Preview the slide and save the file when finished.

Creating interactive conversations

Let's look at pulling together all of the information you've learned in this chapter to create an interactive, expressive conversation between characters and the learner.

You already have the knowledge needed to do this including inserting characters, creating states, adding audio, timing the display of slide objects, and using triggers to create an action. So, let's give it a go!

Follow along...

Be sure to have Exercise 4 - Workplace Compliance open. This exercise works through a simple example of an interactive conversation. Forthcoming exercises will build upon this, adding new functionality and interactivity to the conversation.

1. Switch to **Story View** and double-click on the **3.1 Privacy** slide.

2. Press *Ctrl + D* to duplicate the slide. Rename the new copy as Phone Call.

3. Select the **3.1 Privacy** slide and add an animation to the cell phone by choosing **Animations** and adding an entrance effect of **Spin and Grow**.

4. Add a new textbox and type `The phone is ringing!`. Place this to the right of the phone, make it red, and increase the font size. You may want to switch to a casual font, something like Comic Sans.

5. Select the cell phone and add a trigger to jump to the next slide when the user clicks on the cell phone.

6. Navigate to the **3.2 Phone Call** slide and delete the Scrolling Panel as well as the Google search image.

7. Retitle this slide as `What should John do?`.

8. Insert a speech bubble and add text that says "Hi John. Please provide your consent to monitor this call." Size and format the bubble so that it's pointing from the cell phone and hovering just above it (see the example screenshots at the end of the exercise).

9. Add an entrance animation to the bubble so that it fades in.

10. Insert a character who will be answering the phone. To do this, choose **Insert | Character | Illustrated** and pick **Male 13**, select the **Left** position, and choose a pose of **Sitting at computer with phone**.

11. Move the character to the right side of the white paper image.

12. Add two buttons, one that says "Okay" and the other that says "Why?". Place these buttons vertically in the middle of the slide (see the example screenshots at the end of the exercise).

13. Add a trigger to the **Okay** button that changes the state of the John character to **Alarmed** when clicked.

14. Add a trigger to the **Why?** Button that changes the state of the John character to **Thinking** when clicked.

15. Now let's edit the states of the character by selecting the character, clicking on the **States** panel, and choosing **Edit States**. You'll notice that Storyline automatically added the two new states to the character image.

16. Click on the **Alarmed** state and insert two textboxes.

    ○ **John should not have said that**: Position this above the character and format it so the font is 14 pt and is red.

    ○ **Click the Next button to find out why**: Position this to the right of the character and format it in the same way.

17. Insert a checkmark shape and format it to be green.

18. Click on the **Thinking** state and insert a textbox that says "Good Job! John is right to investigate." Add an X shape and format it red.

19. Press *Ctrl + D* to duplicate this slide and rename the copy as `Wrong`. Navigate to this slide.

20. Delete the buttons and adjust the text as follows:

    1. Change the speech bubble text to "That's great. So let's review some of your personal details..."

    2. Add a new textbox with the following text:

       By not investigating, John doesn't know who he is providing details to or why. This is a privacy and security issue.

    3. Format this to fit near the top of the slide, perhaps in red so that it stands out and reinforces that the learner response was incorrect.

21. Preview this scene by clicking on **Preview** in the ribbon and choosing **This Scene**. While previewing, click on the phone to see the phone call and click on both buttons to see how the states are working. Click on the **Next** button to see the incorrect feedback.

22. Close **Preview** and save the file.

The following screenshots show the previewed results when selecting the right answer:

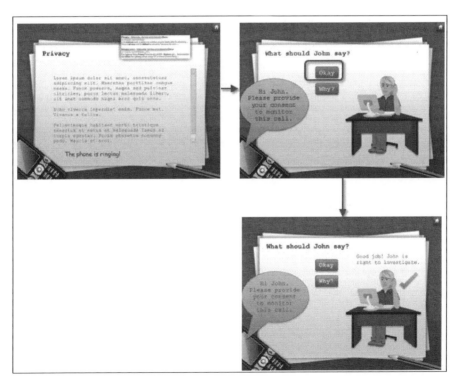

The following screenshots show the previewed results when selecting the wrong answer.

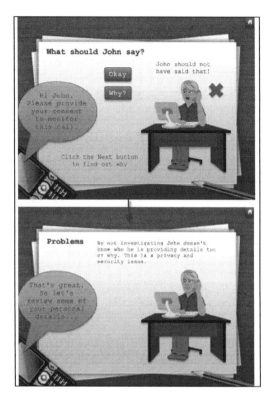

This exercise demonstrated basic interaction techniques. Most interactions are created using the built-in quizzing feature, triggers, and variables to precisely control what information appears and when it appears. As you progress through this book you will have opportunities to put into practice some of the more advanced features of Storyline.

Summary

This chapter introduced some interesting, fun, and easy-to-use features of Storyline that help add a human touch to the courses that you create.

You learned how to add characters into your story and control their expressions, poses, and conversation through states and triggers, another powerful combination in Storyline. Once again, this level of complexity was achieved without complicated programming and without animation skills or design skills.

Einstein once said, "Everything must be made as simple as possible. But not simpler." Creating a human touch is born out of well-constructed and refined content, and this is the content you should be working with in Storyline; just what is needed and no more. Simplification is the hardest part but without it, no matter how much sparkle and shine is added in Storyline, it will lead to uninspiring and ineffectual training.

Bringing out the human touch can be achieved through realistic conversation, situations and practice—just like in real life and Storyline makes this easy to do.

Here are some examples of when you might consider the features you have learned in this chapter to make your course more approachable, interesting, and realistic:

- Use a character as a guide to introduce the course content, duration, navigation, and topic summaries.

- Use a character as a facilitator that can appear when you anticipate the learner is likely to need additional help. This works remarkably well when content is well designed and written to support the learner.

- Use audio with characters to assist in role play scenarios. Audio along with characters is more effective than text speech bubbles alone.

If you have been following along with the exercises so far, you will now have several slides in the `Exercise 4 - Workplace Compliance` file with each slide containing static and interactive content. Even with smaller files like this, it doesn't take long before you need to look at ways to organize content. The next chapter will introduce the concept of layers to help organize and extend slide content.

5

Extending Slide Content

This chapter focuses on a powerful Storyline concept called **layers**. Layers are useful in organizing and extending the slide's content within a single slide as opposed to spreading content over multiple slides. Layers can help optimize your story by reducing the number of overall slides, making for smaller file sizes and faster publishing times.

In this chapter you will learn:

- When and why you might use a layer
- How to create and edit layers
- How to configure the settings of layers
- The techniques for displaying and hiding layers
- To work with built-in interactions that work or complement layers

About layers

If you've used Articulate Studio or PowerPoint previously, you will have noticed that each slide can contain any number of objects that can be placed in front or behind other objects. You can do the same with Storyline by controlling the order of slide objects in the Timeline.

Slide layers are like slide objects that can be layered on top of each other. Think of it like using a transparency sheet on a projector. You can place one transparency at a time on the projector or you can add one on top of the other and keep the information on the bottom transparency visible while adding new information to it. Storyline slide layers can work like this with transparency or can be solid where they do not allow objects on the base layer or other layers to show through.

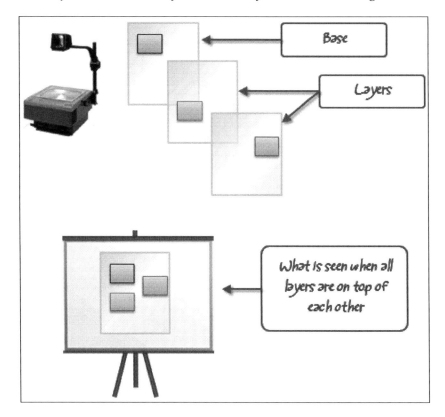

Here's an example that uses a three-tab interaction. To build an interaction like this in Articulate Studio (shown on the left), you would need to use multiple slides, one for each tab, just like placing one transparency at a time on a projector. In Storyline, you could also use multiple slides with hyperlinks to achieve this, however, you might opt to use multiple layers since it would result in one slide instead of three. This is like placing one transparency on top of another, stacking information over multiple levels instead of spreading it over different slides. By using layers, you keep the entire tabbed interaction together on a single slide.

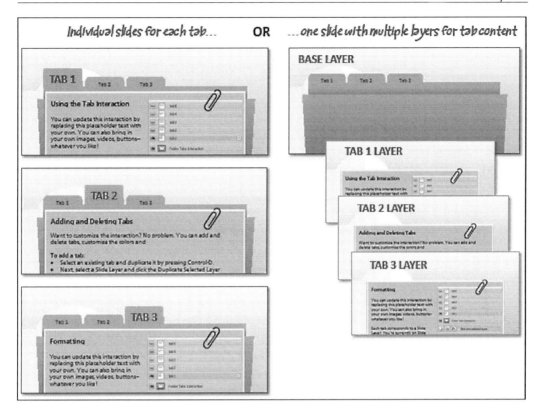

Layers are also useful with rollovers or button clicks to reveal glossary definitions, pop-up tips, hints, and so on. In Articulate Studio, you'd have to create a separate slide for the information that is to be revealed by the rollover or button click. This second slide often contains duplicated information that leads to larger file sizes and increased development time.

There are times when layers might not be so useful, particularly when a single slide has a lot of information in it. For editing and organization, you'll find it easier to spread content-heavy slides over multiple slides. This helps reduce on-screen content, making it easier for the learner to digest and easier for you to edit.

Just like working with regular slides, each layer has its own Timeline, and you can place any number of objects in a layer using all of the regular formatting commands and Storyline features, such as animations and effects.

Some features, such as freeform dragging-and-dropping and zoom (for panning and zooming effects), aren't supported in layers, so you'd need slides instead.

To this point you have been working with just the base layer of a slide. This layer appears by default as soon as the slide starts. All other layers on a slide remain hidden from display until they are triggered to appear. This could be by the click of a button or by a timed event; for example, when a particular image appears on the Timeline, a layer will automatically display. Hiding layers works similarly; you can conceal a layer by a trigger or a timed event.

Adding a layer

Follow these steps to add a layer:

1. Choose **Insert | Slide Layer** from the ribbon or select the **New Layer** icon from the **Slide Layers** panel.

2. The new layer is called **Untitled Layer 1** by default. It's a good habit to give each layer a descriptive name. You can do this by right-clicking on a layer in the **Slide Layers** panel and then renaming it.

Adjusting layers

You may want to hide, duplicate, delete, or create another layer. All of these commands are found at the bottom of the **Slide Layers** panel. By default, all layers except the one you're working on will appear dimmed. If you'd rather see them in full color, you can unmark the box called **Dim non-selected layers** in the **Slide Layers** panel.

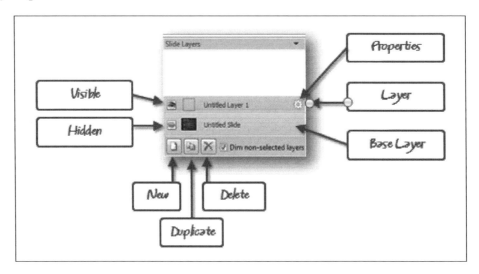

Ordering layers

Slide layers display on top of the base layer. By default, objects on a layer are only visible when the layer is viewed, however, this default can be changed. You can configure a layer so that objects on other layers are visible when the layer is viewed, and when this occurs, objects on other layers will appear in the same layer-order as they are listed in the **Slide Layers** panel, from bottom to top. This is similar to objects on a slide where those that are at the Timeline appear underneath those at the top.

To change the layer order, select a layer in the **Slide Layers** panel and drag it up or down to a different position.

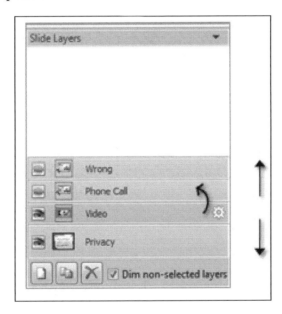

Editing the properties of a layer

Each slide layer can be customized to control how it appears and functions.
Click on the small gear icon to the right of the layer name to display the **Layer
Properties** window. You can also right-click on a layer and choose **Properties**.

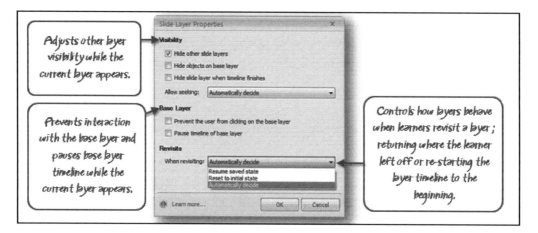

Formatting a layer

Formatting a layer usually involves adding and editing objects on the layer.
In addition to controlling the visibility of other layers, you can also hide or
show all or some of the objects on the base layer. There is also a master slide
that can be used to create consistent formatting between layers.

Adding visibility of base layer objects

Here are the steps to control the visibility of base layer objects:

1. Select a layer and view the Timeline of the layer.

2. Scroll down the Timeline until you see a group named **Base Layer Objects**.

3. Click on the group to expand it and then click on the **Show/Hide** icon (eye)
   to hide or show individual objects on the base layer. You might need to
   expand the height of the Timeline panel or scroll down in the timeline
   to see all of the objects within the group.

 If you'd like to hide all base layer objects, it is faster to do this
through **Layer Properties** and checking the **Hide objects on
base layer** option.

Adding consistency with master layouts

You can create a consistent look and feel for layers, just like you can for slides, by using master layouts.

Later in this book we'll explore quizzing and formatting quiz results using the Feedback Master, for now, it's important to note that Storyline uses the blank layout of the Feedback Master as the default layout for slide layers.

This means you can adjust the blank layout to customize the look and feel of multiple layers. You can also assign different master layouts to different layers. Just like Slide Masters save time and enable consistency between slides, so do Feedback Masters when you have multiple layers in a project that are similarly formatted.

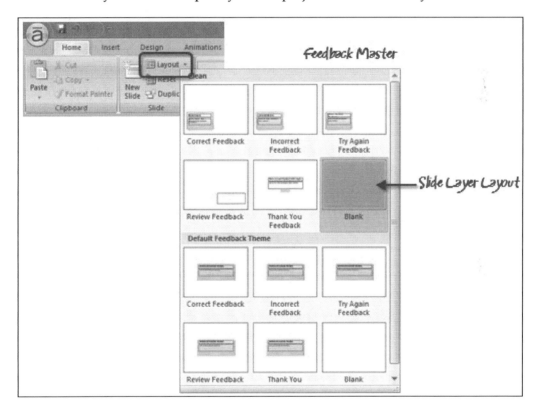

The following are the steps to change or modify the layout for a slide layer:

1. Select the layer you want to change.
2. From the **Home** tab, click on the **Layout** icon or drop-down list. Storyline highlights the Feedback Master layout that is currently being used.

3. You can choose another layout to use, or from the **View** tab, choose **Feedback Master** to change the layout as you would change a Slide Master layout.

 You can adjust the transparency of slide layers by using the **Format Background** option on the slide layout in the Feedback Master that is associated with a layer. By setting a fill color and adjusting the transparency value, this will make objects on the base layer appear dim, similar to a lightbox effect.

Adding content to a layer

You can work with a slide layer in the same way you would work with a regular slide. Each layer has its own Timeline so objects can be timed to appear, and animation effects can be applied. You can even add transitions for each layer.

Using **Layer Properties**, you can control the visibility of other layers and objects on the base layer.

Follow along...

The exercise at the end of *Chapter 4*, *Adding Characters and Audio*, created a file called Exercise 4 - Workplace Compliance. This file should be open in Storyline before continuing. In this exercise, you will optimize and organize the **Privacy** section of the module using layers.

1. Let's take the slides **3.2 Phone Call** and **3.3 Wrong**, and transform them from slides to layers within the slide **3.1 Privacy**. The first step is to add two new layers:

    1. Navigate to slide **3.1 Privacy** (be sure to be in the **Normal** view).
    2. In the **Layers** panel, click on the **New Layer** icon twice.
    3. Rename the first layer to Phone Call by right-clicking on the layer and choosing **Rename**.
    4. Rename the second layer to Wrong.

2. Now let's copy the information from slides 3.2 and 3.3 into the new layers:

    1. Navigate to slide **3.2 Phone Call**, click anywhere in the slide and press *Ctrl + A* to select all objects on the slide. Press *Ctrl + C* to copy the objects.

2. Navigate to slide **3.1 Privacy**, click on the **Phone Call** layer, and press *Ctrl* + *V* to paste the objects.

3. Repeat this for the slide **3.3 Wrong**, and copy all the objects in the **Wrong** layer of the slide **3.1 Privacy**.

4. In preparation for adding triggers to display the new layers, let's make a few content adjustments within the layers:

3. Delete the slides **3.2 Phone Call** and **3.3 Wrong**.

    1. On the slide **3.1 Privacy**, click on the **Phone Call** layer and insert a new textbox and type the following text:

        Click the phone to end the call

    2. Change the text color to red and make the sentence bold.

    3. Move the text so that it appears next to the cell phone and resize the text box so the text spans over two lines.

    4. Press *Ctrl* + *C* to copy.

    5. Click on the **Wrong** layer and press *Ctrl* + *V* to paste the text.

    6. Select the cell phone and then click on the **New Trigger** icon in the **Triggers** panel.

    7. Adjust the trigger so that it jumps to the slide **1.2 Menu** when the user clicks on the cell phone.

    8. In the **Triggers** panel, copy this new trigger by selecting the trigger and clicking on the **Copy** icon at the bottom of the **Triggers** panel.

    9. Select the **Phone Call** layer, select the cell phone, and click on the **Paste** icon in the **Triggers** panel.

    10. Select the **Wrong** layer and adjust the explanation text as well as the speech bubble so that it looks similar to the following sample screenshot.

    11. While still viewing the **Wrong** layer, adjust the timing of the two objects in the Timeline as follows:

    12. Move the textbox **Textbox 1** (this is the text that appears below the word **Problems**) so that it begins at the 1.5 second mark.

    13. Move the speech bubble **Caption 1** so that it begins at the .5 second mark.

    14. Select the **Phone Call** layer and adjust the following three objects in the Timeline as follows:

15. Move the **Why?** and **Okay** buttons so that they begin at the 1 second mark.

16. Move the **What should John say?** textbox to the beginning of the timeline.

4. Save the file under a new name of Exercise 5 - Workplace Compliance.

Showing and hiding a layer

Layers remain hidden until they are triggered to display. Most often this is because of something the learner did, a mouse click or hovering over an object. For example, there might be a highlighted word on a slide, when the mouse is hovered over the word, a definition appears and, when moved away from the word, the definition disappears. The hover action invokes the display of a layer and moving the mouse away triggers the hiding of the layer.

Displaying a layer by mouse action

Follow these steps to display a layer by mouse action:

1. Select the object that will trigger the display of a layer and choose **Insert | Trigger** from the ribbon or click on the **New Trigger** icon in the **Triggers** panel.

2. Under the **Action** drop-down menu, select **Show Layer**.

3. Under **Layer**, select the layer you want to display.

4. Under **When**, select **User clicks** or **Mouse hovered over**.

5. Click on **OK**.

Hiding a layer

By default, if a layer is triggered by the **Mouse hovered over** option, it will automatically be hidden when the mouse moves away. You can adjust this by de-selecting the **Restore on mouse leave** option in the trigger wizard.

Alternatively, if the learner clicks on an object to display a layer, they will typically need to do something to close the layer, for example, clicking on an object in the layer such as an **X** (close) icon. You could also set a layer to automatically hide once the layer timeline has completed. For this to work properly, you will need to adjust the overall duration of the timeline to allow enough time for the learner to complete whatever activity is on the layer.

1. Select the layer you want to adjust.

2. To make an object clickable in order to close a layer, perform the following steps:

    1. Select an object on the layer that the learner will click to hide the layer.

    2. Add a new trigger to this object and choose **Hide Layer** in the **Action** drop down.

    3. In the **Layer** drop-down menu, select **This Layer**.

    4. In the **When** drop-down menu, select **User clicks** and make sure that the object they should click on is selected in the **Object** drop down.

    5. Click on **OK**.

3. To make the layer automatically hide when the Timeline completes, perform the following steps:

    1. Adjust the duration of the layer timeline to allow enough time for the learner to complete the layer activity (reading or other interaction).

    2. Click on the **New Trigger** icon in the **Triggers** panel and select **Hide Layer** under **Action**.

    3. Choose **This Layer** in the **Layer** drop down and choose **Timeline Ends** in the **When** drop down.

    4. Select the current layer in the **Object** drop down.

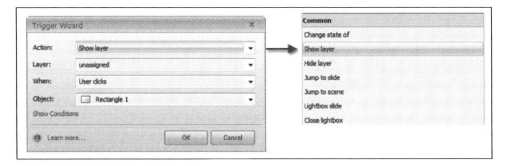

Follow along...

Continuing with `Exercise 5 - Workplace Compliance`, you will now add triggers to control how and when each layer is displayed and concealed.

1. Navigate to the slide **3.1 Privacy** and click on the **Privacy** layer to ensure you are viewing the base layer.

    1. Click on the cell phone and adjust the trigger so that it shows the layer **Phone Call** when the user clicks on the phone.

    2. Click on the **Phone Call** layer, and then click on the **Okay** button and change the trigger so that it shows the layer **Wrong** when the user clicks on the button.

    3. On the same layer, click on the **Why?** button and change the trigger so that the character **John 1** changes its state to **Thinking** when the user clicks on the button.

    4. Click on the **Privacy** layer and select the entire second paragraph that displays in the scroll box on the slide. Type the following text as its replacement:

    Let's take a look at how Bob and his team deal with privacy concerns

2. The original template contains a video in a layer on this slide. Let's link to it. Select the words "take a look" from the sentence just typed and select **Insert | Hyperlink** from the ribbon.

3. Adjust the trigger so that it shows the layer called **Video** when the user clicks on these words.

    1. Select the **Design** tab and from the **Colors** drop down, click on **Custom 1**. This will format the hyperlink to black instead of blue.

    2. Click on the **Video** layer, then click on the red **X** (close) button. Notice the trigger that is assigned. This trigger instructs Storyline to hide this layer when clicked and is a common method of closing a layer and returning to the base layer.

    3. Save the file.

    4. Preview the entire project. Test navigating to the **Privacy** section and working with the layers. Remember that clicking on the cell phone will return to the main menu.

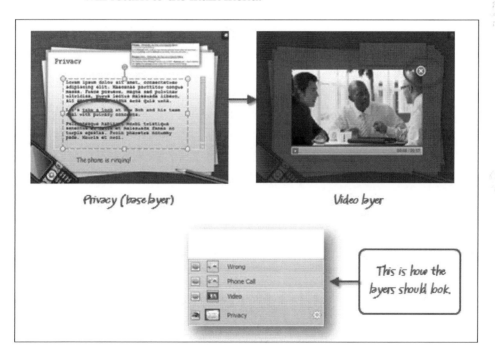

Privacy (base layer)

Video layer

This is how the layers should look.

Features that extend a slide's content

This section reviews features that work with layers or that can help you organize and extend a slide's content. As well as these, keep in mind that any object on a slide can be made to work with layers (showing or hiding them), using triggers.

Hotspots

Hotspots are shapes that can be added to a slide and respond similar to a button. Hotspots do not have states and they are invisible. When the learner clicks or hovers over a hotspot, something is triggered; often this will be some kind of information pop up contained in a slide layer or on another slide.

Hotspots are useful when you have an image on the slide that contains irregular shapes. Hotspots can be made to be any shape that can be overlaid on top of other slide objects.

In the following example, there is diagram that was imported into Storyline as a single, large image. Within the image are various irregular shapes and those shapes are made interactive by inserting hotspots on top of the background diagram.

Adding a hotspot

The following are the steps to add a hotspot:

1. Choose **Insert | Hotspot** from the ribbon.

2. Choose **Oval**, **Rectangle**, or **Freeform** and draw the hotspot on the slide.

3. By default a trigger is created to display a layer. Choose the layer to display or change the trigger to perform a different action such as navigating to a different slide.

Markers

Markers are a built-in way to quickly extend slide content by using click-and-reveal effects. Markers are useful when you want to provide context-sensitive information or when you want to reduce the volume of on-screen content, allowing the learner to reveal the content by interacting with a slide object.

Markers are inserted just like shapes and can be placed anywhere on the slide. You can have as many markers as you would like to have on a slide. Markers can display text or icons and can be formatted in terms of size, style, and animation effects.

The following example shows markers being used to display map information:

Markers do not use layers to display content though it looks as if they do. The content is built within the marker and isn't displayed on a layer or in a state.

Adding a marker

The following are the steps to add a marker:

1. Choose **Insert | Marker** from the ribbon.

2. Select the type of marker from the gallery of marker options.

3. Click on the slide where you would like the marker to appear.

4. Enter the **Title** and **Description**.

5. Format the text and resize or move the marker as you would resize or move a slide object.

6. Add media to the marker by clicking on the marker and choosing the **Format** tab.

7. Adjust the way a marker looks by choosing the **Format** tab and adjusting the marker and label styles, icon appearance, and animation effect.

Follow along...

Continuing with `Exercise 5 - Workplace Compliance`, you will enhance the course by bringing the calculator to life.

1. Navigate to the slide **2.1 Business Conduct** and switch to the **Normal** view.

2. Zoom in to the slide so that you can clearly see the calculator by dragging the **Zoom** slider in the lower-left corner of the window.

3. Once the calculator is in full view, select **Insert | Hotspot** from the ribbon and choose **Freeform** as the shape.

4. A crosshair will appear in place of the mouse pointer. Move the crosshair to the upper-left corner of the equal button and click once. Repeat this for each of the other corners. At the final corner, the hotspot should fill in transparent green. If not, double-click in the upper-left corner of the equal button to make certain it does.

5. Add a new layer by clicking on the **New Layer** icon at the bottom of the **Layers** panel and rename this layer to be `Display`.

6. Click on the **Display** layer to make it visible. The calculator on the base layer will appear dimmed.

7. Insert a rectangle about the same size as the display area where the total values on the calculator appear. Rotate the rectangle slightly so that it aligns with the display area. Fill the rectangle with a semi-transparent color with a border and glow.

8. Add the text AT RISK to the rectangle, sizing it so that it fits properly and is white or black in color.

9. Since the hotspot will be invisible to the learner, let's add a marker that instructs the learner to click on the equal button.

   1. Select **Insert | Marker** from the ribbon and choose the left arrow (top-left marker in the **Markers** library).

   2. Click to the right of the equal sign on the calculator to place the marker.

   3. Click in the title placeholder textbox and type Are we at risk?.

   4. Click in the description placeholder and type Click the equal button to find out.

   5. Under the **Format** tab within **Label Styles**, choose a light green style for the marker textbox.

   6. Under **Marker Styles**, select solid green for the marker color.

   7. Resize the text to be more readable at 12 pt.

   8. Reduce the size of the marker text box so it tightly fits around the text (as shown in the example screenshot).

10. Next, let's add a marker to inform the learner what the purpose of the display area of the calculator is.

    1. Select **Insert | Marker** from the ribbon and choose the question mark (in the **Help** section of the **Markers** library).

    2. Click to the left of the display area on the calculator to place the marker.

    3. Click anywhere in the title placeholder and type Risk Calculation.

    4. Click anywhere in the description placeholder and type Risk rises when our conduct is not aligned with our corporate expectations of proper conduct.

    5. Change the marker textbox to light red and add a solid red for the marker color.

    6. Resize the text to be more readable and reduce the marker textbox to fit around the text (as shown in the example screenshot).

    7. Click on the outer edge of the marker textbox, hold-and-drag the mouse in a circle around the marker to reposition the textbox. When you find an appropriate position, release the mouse.

11. Save the project and then preview the slide to test the hotspot and markers.

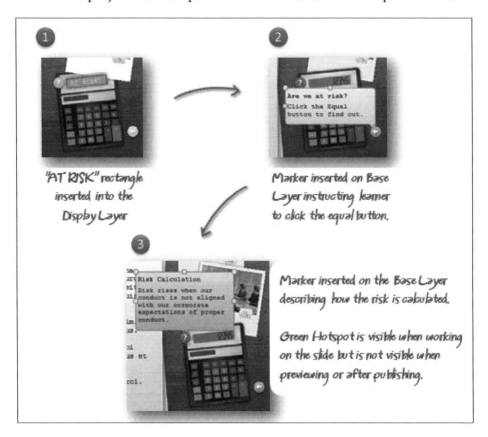

Button sets

Button sets allow you to make objects behave like radio buttons where the learner is able to select one object at a time out of a group of objects. You can have as many button sets on a single slide as you like.

Here's an example. You have three questions on a slide, each requiring the learner to pick just one of the options (the options could come in the form of built-in buttons, images, shapes, captions, characters, and so on). You would create three button sets, one for each of the sets of options. The learner would then be able to select one option for each question. Without a button set, the learner would be able to select all options or, with just one button set, the learner would be able to pick just one option out of all the options across all the questions.

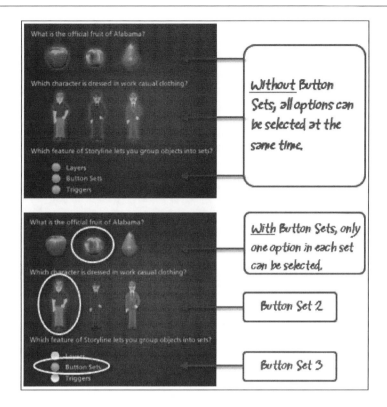

Without Button Sets, all options can be selected at the same time.

With Button Sets, only one option in each set can be selected.

Button Set 2

Button Set 3

Turning a set of objects into a button set

Follow these steps:

1. Select the objects you want to turn into a button set.

2. Right-click and choose **Button Set**.

3. Choose either **Button set 1** (this is the default name for the first button set) or choose **New set** and type a name.

4. If the objects don't have a **Selected** state, Storyline will create one that you can view and edit by clicking on the object and then the **States** panel.

5. Preview the slide to test that only one item at a time can be selected from the button set.

Radio buttons will automatically become part of **Button set 1**. If you are grouping other objects into a button set on the same slide, you will want to choose **New set**, otherwise they will also become part of **Button Set 1**.

Follow along...

Continuing with `Exercise 5 - Workplace Compliance`, you'll enhance the course with the addition of a tab interaction and a button set in the **Security** section.

1. Navigate to the slide **4.1 Security** and be sure to be in the **Normal** view.

2. Let's start by inserting a prebuilt tab interaction and then customizing it to suit our needs. To do this, follow these steps:

   1. Select **Insert | New Slide** from the ribbon.

   2. From the **Template** drop down, choose **Top Interactions**.

   3. The interaction to insert is **Folder Tabs**, locate this interaction and select it.

   4. Choose **Current Scene** from the **Insert into scene** drop down and click on **Import**.

3. Format the newly inserted slide so that its theme matches the other slides in the course. To do this, click on the **4.2 Folder Tabs** slide and select the **Design** tab from the ribbon. Choose the **Desktop** design theme.

4. Change the title from **Folder Tabs Interaction** to **Security Issues**.

5. Retitle each of the tabs as follows:

   ○ From **Tab 1** to `Email`

   ○ From **Tab 2** to `Passwords`

   ○ From **Tab 3** to `WIFI`

   ○ From **Tab 4** to `Stolen PC`

   ○ From **Tab 5** to `Knowledge Check`

6. Change the paper label that is held by a paper clip to **Take a moment to learn more about our most concerning security issues**.

7. The content within each tab is prepopulated with sample text and images. This content appears in a separate layer for each tab. For this exercise, let's keep the sample content for all tabs except the last tab. Click on the **Tab 5** layer to view this layer.

8. Let's create a simple quiz using two sets of radio buttons.

1. Change the title to Do you know? (as shown in the following screenshot).

2. Highlight all of the remaining sample text and replace it with the following:

What is the most frequent security breach?

3. Press the *Enter* key five to six times and type the following:
   What is the most common error when handling files?

4. Format the text so that it is red.

5. Choose **Insert | Button** and select **Radio Button Style 1**.

6. Click beneath the first question to place the radio button.

7. Right-click on the button and choose **Edit Text**.

8. Type `Password Sharing`.

9. Click to select the button and press *Ctrl + C* to copy it.

10. Press *Ctrl + V* to paste it. Move it to the right of the first button.

11. Edit the text so that it says **Lost or Stolen Laptops**.

12. Press *Ctrl + V* three times and move all of the copies below the second question.

13. Select all copies and place them into a new button set by right-clicking, and choosing **Button Set** and then **New Set**. Type the name `Button Set 2` and click on **OK**.

14. Space out each of the three radio buttons for the second question and in the **Home** or **Format** tab, choose **Align** and then select the **Left Align** option followed by **Distribute Vertically**.

15. Adjust the text of each radio button from **Password Sharing** to:
    ○ **Not backing up files**
    ○ **Sharing with unauthorized people**
    ○ **Inappropriate file names**

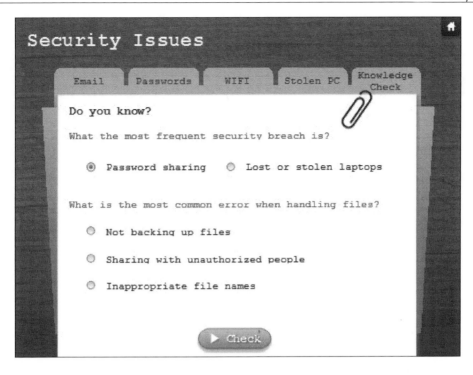

9. Now that the quiz has been created, let's highlight the correct responses and create a new layer to display this (keep in mind this sample quiz is not a scored or recorded quiz, rather, it's an example of using button sets for less formal knowledge checks).

    1. Insert two ovals, making them green so that they stand out, and placing/sizing one to highlight the first response in the first question and the other to highlight the second response in the second question (as shown in the following screenshot).

    2. Select both ovals and cut them from the slide.

    3. Add a new layer and name it Check.

4. Select the **Check** layer and paste the ovals into this layer. By creating the ovals in the **Tab 5** layer, you were able to see correct positioning. Once on the **Check** layer, you cannot see other layers by default, making it difficult to correctly position each of the ovals.

5. Display the **Tab 5** layer and choose **Insert | Button** and select a button style.

6. Click near the bottom center of the slide to insert the button. Format the button to be green, adding a right arrow icon and the word Check.

7. In the **Triggers** panel, click on the **Add trigger** link for the newly created button and adjust it so that when the user clicks, it shows the **Check** layer.

10. Save the file and preview the current slide to test the tab interaction and knowledge check.

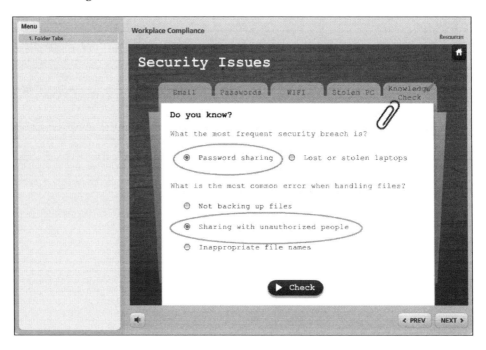

Lightbox

The lightbox feature overlays content from one or more slides on top of the current slide. Lightboxes don't work with layers, but are included in this section to demonstrate another way that you can extend slide content.

In the following example, content from a slide can be viewed from the photo gallery slide without navigating away from the photo gallery. This could have been set up with each photo on a different layer, but in this case the same effect is achieved by adding each photo to a separate slide and using lightboxes to bring the content into the gallery slide. It's a matter of preference as to which method you choose, but in this case, the lightbox feature may save time since it automatically dims the current slide and includes a close button without any extra development effort. Furthermore features that can't be used on a layer, such as viewing narration notes, can be used with this approach.

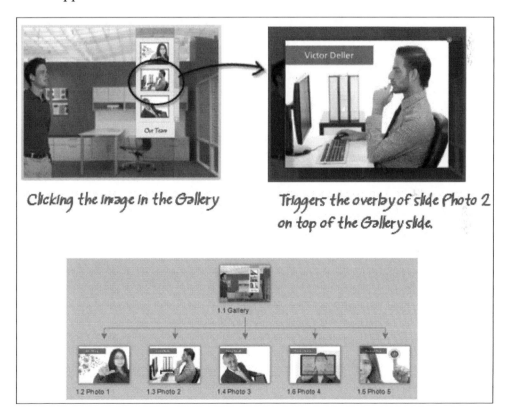

Clicking the image in the Gallery

Triggers the overlay of slide Photo 2 on top of the Gallery slide.

Triggering the display of a lightbox

Here are the steps needed to trigger the display of a lightbox:

1. On the object that will invoke the lightbox, select **Insert | Trigger** from the ribbon.

2. In the **Action** drop down, select **Lightbox slide**, select the slide to place in a lightbox, decide when this occurs, usually this will be **User Clicks**, and select the object to click.

3. You can also include navigation controls within the lightbox display to allow the learner to navigate through more than one slide while viewing in the lightbox.

4. Click on **OK** and preview the entire project.

If you preview just the current slide, the lightbox slide will not appear when previewing. This is because it is calling up another slide that is out of the preview range. Be sure to preview the entire project or scene where the lighbox slide is located.

Follow along...

Continuing with `Exercise 5 - Workplace Compliance`, you'll enhance the course with the addition of a lightbox effect.

1. As a final step, let's place the new tab interaction within a lightbox.

   1. Navigate back to the slide **4.1 Security**.

   2. Insert a button near the bottom center of the slide.

     3. Format the button to be green, adding a right arrow icon and the word `More`.

     4. In the **Triggers** panel, click on the **Add trigger** link and, in the **Triggers** wizard, change the **Action** to **Lightbox** in the **Next** slide.

2. Save the file and preview the current scene to test the lightbox.

3. You are now finished with this sample compliance course. You may want to take some time to clean up the course by renaming objects, adjusting animations, and formatting. Save any changes made and preview the entire course to review all of the work you have done to this point.

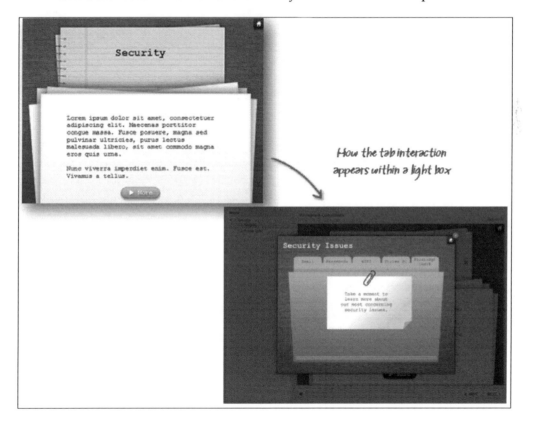

Summary

Layers are particularly helpful for slides that contain interactive content, such as tabbed interactions and pop-up information. Layers can prevent unnecessary duplication of slides while allowing you to keep content and interactions together, making it easier to organize and manage your project.

Deciding when to use a layer instead of an additional slide requires some experimenting. A general rule of thumb is, if there's a lot of content on a slide or if some of the content doesn't naturally belong on the slide (that is, different topics), then using multiple slides is better; this approach can help organize topics and make content editing simpler.

Despite the convenience of having layers within a slide, there are drawbacks in that some features don't work in layers. This should be considered as part of your design planning.

You've reached the point where you've learned the basics about core authoring concepts in Storyline including triggers, states, and layers. These features are fundamental to Storyline and practicing using them often (as well as other features like templates, animations, characters, and button sets) will improve your ability to finesse content and control interaction so that your courses respond exactly how you planned.

In the next chapter, we'll explore some additional ways with which you can transform relatively static material into intelligent interactions that respond to the actions of the learner.

6

Using Variables to Customize the Learning Experience

In this chapter, we'll explore techniques you can employ to draw the learner into your course using Storyline variables to collect, evaluate, and respond to learner actions. Variables are a powerful and optional method of enhancing the level of interactivity in your courses.

In this chapter you will learn:

- What Storyline variables are
- How to create, name, and edit variables
- Collecting and displaying variable content
- Data Entry
- Evaluating variable content
- Creating actions based on variable content
- Restricting advancements until a condition is met
- Tracking and displaying progress

Storyline variables

If you've had exposure to a programming language then you will find the concept of variables familiar. Almost all programming languages make use of them. Variables are also found in day-to-day applications, such as Microsoft Office.

For example, in Microsoft Word you can create a mail merge; this involves a list of names and addresses, and printing one form letter for each of the names. It appears as though the letter is personalized, however, the letter remains the same while the addressee changes. This bit of automation couldn't be possible without variables; one for the first name, one for the last name, and one for the address. Variables act as placeholders that temporarily hold information.

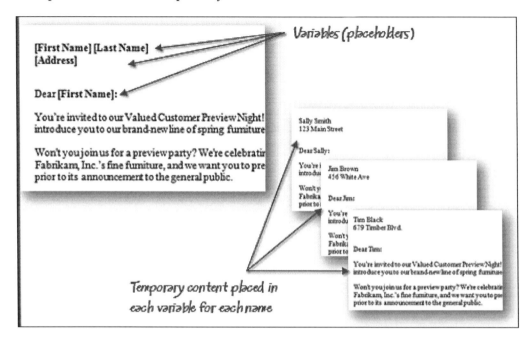

In Storyline, variables are used to do the same thing and more. A simple example is prompting the learner for their name. After typing their name, it is temporarily stored in a variable. Later on you can use the information in the variable to personalize the course content (Hello Sally, Welcome back Bob, Good job Joan, and so on).

There are several ways that information can be placed into a variable. One is by learner input, for example, entering their name. Another is for you to set a default value for a variable; this is often the case for true/false variables. This value can then be adjusted, based on an action from the learner.

For example, a variable that currently has its value set to nothing can be set to **Agree** if the learner clicks on a certain button, or **Don't agree** by clicking on another button, as shown in the following screenshot:

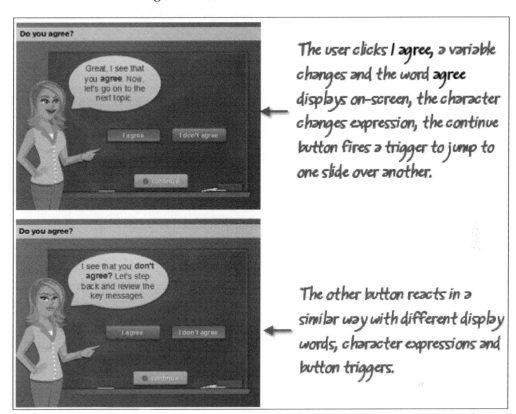

Variables open up an endless variety of customization and personalization options that help create engaging and responsive e-learning experiences. What's really great about variables is just how interesting it is to work with them, and how easy it is to create powerful results. Let's take a look!

Types of variables

There are three types of variables available in Storyline:

- `True/False`: This type of variable is sometimes known as a Boolean variable. Unlike numeric or text variables, they can have one of two states: on or off. This type of variable can be used for things such as toggling buttons based on user input, detecting learner activity such as where a user is in a course, or seeking acknowledgement such as user agreement.

- `Number`: This type of variable contains numeric values only and can be manipulated using basic math operations (add, subtract, multiply, and divide). Number variables are often used for scores and number of attempts.

- `Text`: This type of variable can contain any value: numbers, letters, spaces, and special characters. All information is treated as text and cannot be manipulated like a number variable can.

As is the case with all variables, the information contained within is temporary only. For example, you may have a variable called opinion and use this to ask the learner for their opinion at several points throughout a course. When first asked, the learner enters some information, and this is stored in the variable. The next time you ask, the learner types something new which overwrites whatever was previously stored in the variable.

 Variables and object states seem similar but states can only hold information for the current slide while variables can hold data across the entire project.

Follow along...

This exercise will involve creating a new project based on a prebuilt Articulate-supplied template. You will need access to the Internet in order to download the template. The goal for this exercise is to create and format the project to get it ready for use with variables in later exercises.

Part 1 – creating a new project and adjusting the slides

In order to create a new project and adjust the slides, follow these steps:

1. Start a new project in Storyline. You will have a single, blank slide in the story.

2. Let's add content to this project, and a custom look and feel by leveraging a prebuilt template. To do this, click on **Insert | New Slide** from the ribbon.

3. Near the top center, click on **Download free templates**. This will open your browser and display a page containing several free Articulate-built templates. Look for the template named **Business Circles**, click to select it, then choose **Download this file** (you will need to sign up for a free Articulate account to download the templates).

4. When prompted to **Save** or **Open**, choose **Open** to open the template in Storyline.

5. If prompted to make the file writable, click on **Yes**.

6. The scenes and slides in the template now appear. For this exercise you will only need a few of the slides. Using *Ctrl* + click, navigate to the following slides:

   ° The **Menu** slide

   ° **Module 1**: the first 2 untitled slides

   ° **Module 2**: the first 2 untitled slides

   ° **Module 3**: the first 2 untitled slides

7. Ensure that **Same as imported template** is selected from the drop-down list. Insert a **Scene** menu in the lower left corner.

8. Click on **Import**.

9. In **Story View**, remove the first untitled scene that contains a single, blank slide by right-clicking on the scene and choosing **Delete**.

10. Let's change the theme color by selecting the **Design** tab and from the **Colors** drop-down menu, select the **Office** color theme.

11. Rename the first slide in each of the module scenes from **Untitled Slide** to **Intro,** and rename the second slide in each of the scenes from **Untitled Slide** to **Details**.

 It's a good practice to rename slides using a descriptive name. Slide names appear in the menu when the course is previewed and published. You can change slide names later but it's more efficient to get into the habit of naming slides the way you would want users to see them, as you create the slides.

12. Double-click on **1.1 Menu** to view it in **Normal View**.

13. Save the file as Exercise 6- Sales Training.

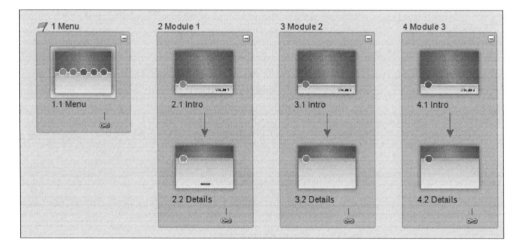

Part 2 – Adjusting formatting

Let's continue making some adjustments:

1. Navigate to slide **1.1 Menu** then switch to **Slide Master View**.

2. Delete the last two circles that appear in the center of the slide.

3. Select the remaining three circles and group them by pressing *Ctrl* + *G*.

4. Align the circles in the center of the slide by choosing **Format** | **Align** | **Align Center** from the **Slide Master** menu.

5. Press *Shift* + *Ctrl* + *G* to ungroup the circles.

6. Navigate to the first circle (orange) and from the **Timeline** panel, choose the **States** tab, and edit **States**. Change the **Visited** state to a light grey fill, click on the **New State** icon, and name it **Completed**. Insert a checkmark shape and place this beside the circle (this will be used to indicate the section is complete in a later exercise).

7. Repeat the step above for the other two circles.

8. Adjust the trigger for each of the circles so that each trigger jumps to the appropriate **Intro** slide (orange jumps to **2.1 Intro**, blue jumps to **3.1 Intro,** and purple jumps to **4.1 Intro**).

9. Navigate to the first **Module 1** layout from the left side panel. This layout shows an orange circle on the left side of the slide. Select the orange circle on the slide and change the trigger to jump to **1.1 Menu**.

10. Repeat this for the first **Module 2** layout and **Module 3** layout.

11. Press *Ctrl + S* to save the file.

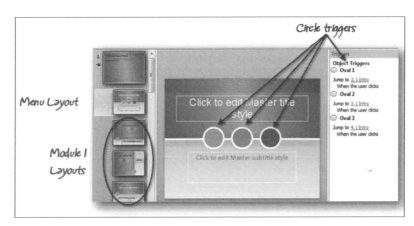

Part 3 – adding new slides and previewing functionality

Let's finish the initial adjustments to this project:

1. Switch to **Story View** and navigate to slide **1.1 Menu**.

2. Change the **Slide Advances** setting in the slide panel to **By User**.

3. Let's add two new slides to the project and prep them for later exercises:

    1. Press *Ctrl + D* to duplicate slide **1.1 Menu** and rename the copy to **Start**.

2. Right-click on slide **1.2 Start**, choose **Layout,** and change the layout to be the final **Module 1** (orange circle) layout.

3. Switch to **Normal View** and type **Please enter your name** for the title on the slide, and delete the placeholder box that appears in the center of the slide.

4. Switch back to **Story View** and add a new scene to the project.

5. Name the scene **End** and rename slide **5.1 Untitled Slide** to **You're Done**.

6. View **5.1 You're Done** in **Normal View**, enter a title of **You're Done!** And add the following text in the placeholder below the three circles: **Great job! You've completed this series and can now move on to Level II**.

4. In **Normal View**, navigate to **1.2 Menu**, enter a title **Welcome!** and introductory text below the three circles as: **There are three modules in this course. Complete each module then click on the Next button to continue**.

5. Press *Ctrl + S* to save the file.

6. Preview the entire project and test navigation; clicking each of the circles should navigate to the respective module section, and from there clicking on the colored circle should return to the menu. If this doesn't work, re-examine the triggers setup in the **Master Layout** for the menu and module layouts.

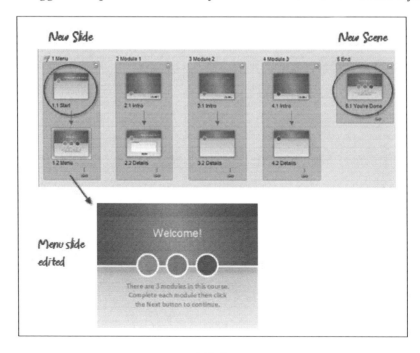

Creating variables

Creating a variable involves defining a unique name, selecting the type, and setting the initial value (or initial content) for the variable:

1. In the **Triggers** panel, click on **Manage project variables (X)**
2. Click on the **Create a new variable** icon
3. Name your variable
4. Set the variable type
5. Set the initial value of the variable if it is a number or true/false variable
6. Click on **OK**

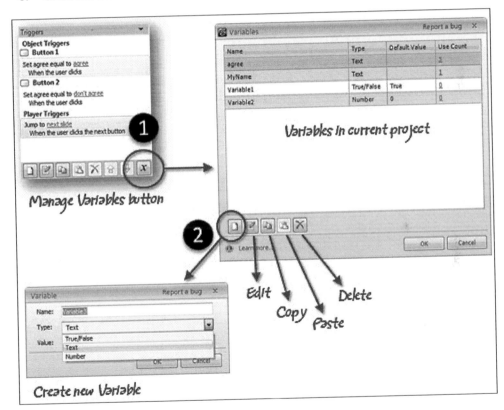

All variables must be uniquely named with no spaces or special characters, and the name of a variable is case sensitive. Once a variable is created its type cannot be changed.

Using variables

For variables to be useful, they need to contain some form of content whether that is text, numbers, or true/false logic.

One common way of populating variables is through button clicks; where the learner clicks on a button and by doing so a variable is populated with specific content. This is easy to set up in Storyline; just create a trigger on a button but instead of jumping to a slide, or showing a layer when the user clicks, you instruct Storyline to adjust the content (referred to as the value) of a variable.

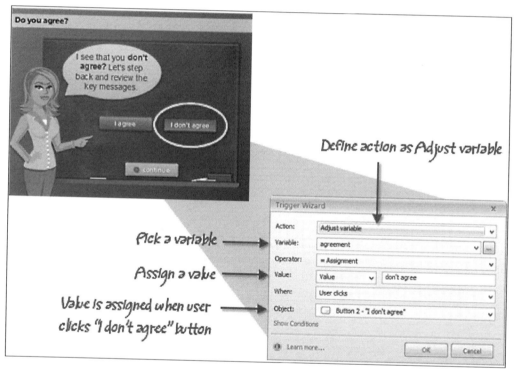

When working with variables you will want to ensure they are behaving the way you intend, and contain the information you expect.

Being able to see what's stored in a variable is very helpful for testing purposes, and you can do this by inserting a reference to a variable. This is inserted on a slide like a normal textbox where the textbox contains the name of the variable surrounded by percentage symbols %variablename%. When previewing or publishing, the reference changes to show the actual content stored in the variable.

When using references for testing, you'll just temporarily insert the reference, and then remove it once you're satisfied the variable is working as expected. The technique of inserting references is not just for testing though. It's also the way you display information to the learner as part of your course content (for example, learner name, current location, progress, scores, and so on).

Inserting a reference to a variable

In order to insert a reference to a variable, follow these steps:

1. From the **Insert** tab, choose **Textbox** and click once on the slide.

2. Go back to the **Insert** tab and choose **Reference** from the **Text** section of the ribbon. This displays a list of project variables. Select the appropriate variable.

3. Click **OK**.

4. Format the textbox as you normally would to adjust font color and size.

5. Preview the slide to view the current content of the variable.

Data Entry

The **Data Entry** feature lets you populate a variable with information the learner types in, for example, learner name, learner thoughts on a topic, or information needed from the learner to complete an activity or exercise. **Data Entry** boxes can accept text or number content, and you can add as many as you'd like to a slide

There are three components to consider when working with **Data Entry** boxes:

- First, the box that will contain the information that the learner types.
- Second, a trigger that sends the typed input into the variable.
- Third, a reference to display the typed input (variable contents). This can be the default of clicking away from the **Data Entry** box but is most often based on a click of a button.

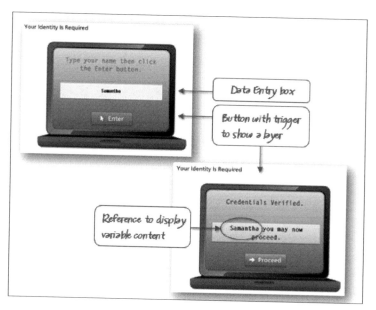

Inserting a Data Entry box

The following steps allow you to insert a Data Entry box:

1. From the **Insert** tab, choose **Data Entry** from the **Interactive Objects** area of the ribbon.
2. Navigate to **Text Entry** or **Number Entry**.
3. Click-and-drag on the slide to draw the **Data Entry** box.
4. Default text appears inside the box and this can be adjusted to provide instructions for the learner, or removed altogether.
5. Format the **Data Entry** box as you would any other textbox.
6. Preview the slide to see how the **Data Entry** box appears and to test its ability to accept data.

When adding a **Data Entry** box, a new trigger is created that defines a variable, and places the typed input into the variable when the **control loses focus** (that is, when the learner clicks away from the **Data Entry** box).

By default, your new variable will be named **TextEntry**. You can change the name of the assigned variable to something more descriptive by double-clicking on **the Mange Project Variables (X) button in the lower right of the Triggers panel, clicking on the TextEntry name, typing a new name and clicking OK.**

Follow along...

Continuing with `Exercise 6- Sales Training`. This exercise will set up project variables to capture and display the learner name, and the response to a question. This will be done using **Data Entry** boxes and variable references.

Part 1 – adding a Data Entry box to solicit learner thoughts

Let's start with the following steps:

1. The first task for this exercise is to create project variables that you will use in this exercise and the next. To create a variable, click on the **Manage project variables (X)** button in the lower right corner of the `Triggers` panel.

2. Create the following new variables:

   - `LearnerName`, text, no default value
   - `Mod1Complete`, true/false, default value set to **False**
   - `Mod2Complete`, true/false, default value set to **False**
   - `Mod3Complete`, true/false, default value set to **False**
   - `Thoughts`, text, no default value

3. Switch to **Normal View** and enter the title **Module 1** on slide 2.1. Repeat this for **Module 2** and **Module 3** on slides 3.1 and 4.1 respectively.

4. Navigate to slide **2.2 Details** and type **What do you think?** for the title.

5. Insert a **Data Entry** box in the lower portion of the slide by navigating to **Insert | Data Entry | Text Entry** from the menu, and draw a box on the slide where the **Data Entry** box will reside (this can be adjusted later).

6. Change the text inside the box to **Type your thoughts here,** and format the box similar to how it appears in the image at the end of this exercise.

7. In the `Triggers` panel, double-click to edit the **TextEntry** trigger, and change the variable to **Thoughts** as the variable to use to store what the learner types in this box.

8. Add a new layer to this slide called **Feedback** and go to the layer.

9. On the left side of the slide, insert a new textbox and type **What you said…** in bold, blue, and 14pt font.

10. Below this, insert another textbox, and type `%Thoughts%` to insert a reference to the **Thoughts** variable.

11. Select both the textboxes, press *Ctrl + D* to duplicate, and position the copies on the right side of the slide. Change the first textbox to **What the experts say…** and replace the second textbox with placeholder content by typing `=lorem()` and pressing *Enter*.

12. Click on the base layer and insert a new button that will submit user input, and display the **Feedback Layer**. Select **Insert | Button** and choose a button style. Add the word **Submit** as text on the button. Format the button to blue and place it beneath the **Data Entry** box.

13. In the **Triggers** panel, adjust the button trigger so that it shows the **Feedback Layer** when the user clicks on the **Submit** button.

14. Select the **Feedback Layer** and from the **Timeline** panel, click on the **Base Layer Objects** group to expand it, then click on the **Show/Hide** icon (eye) to hide **Button 1** and **TextEntry** trigger from being visible in this layer. You might need to expand the height of the **Timeline** panel, or scroll down in the **Timeline** panel to see all the objects within the group.

15. Switch back to the **Base Layer** and press *Ctrl + S* to save the file.

16. Preview this slide to test entering text and view the contents of the
    Thoughts variable.

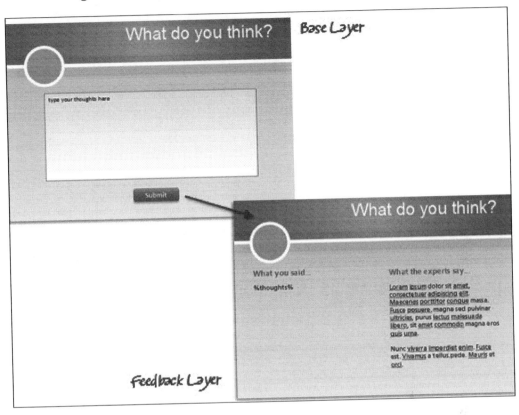

Part 2 – adding a Data Entry box to collect a learner name

To add a Data Entry box to collect a learner name proceed, with the following steps:

1. Navigate to slide **1.1 Start** and add a **Data Entry** box to the center of the slide similar to the image at the end of this exercise.

2. Double-click on the **TextEntry** trigger in the **Triggers** panel, and go to **LearnerName** from the **Set Variable** drop-down menu.

3. Add a textbox to provide instructions to click on **Next** to continue, and place this below the **Data Entry** box.

4. Navigate to **1.2 Menu** and insert a space and then %LearnerName% after the word **Welcome** in the title. You may want to resize the textbox to be the full width of the slide.

5. Save the project.

6. Preview this scene to test entering a name and view it on the **Menu** slide.

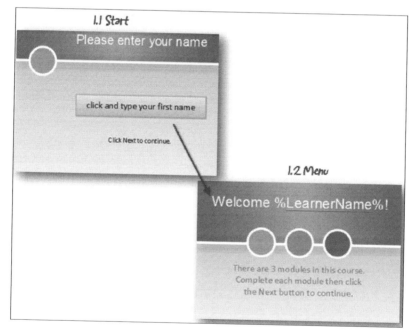

Refining action based on conditions

Storyline conditions provide a way for you to evaluate the content of a variable based on certain criteria such as equal to, not equal to, greater than, and less than. You can add more than one condition by creating an **AND** or an **OR** statement.

Conditions can be included on a trigger by clicking on the **Show Conditions** option.

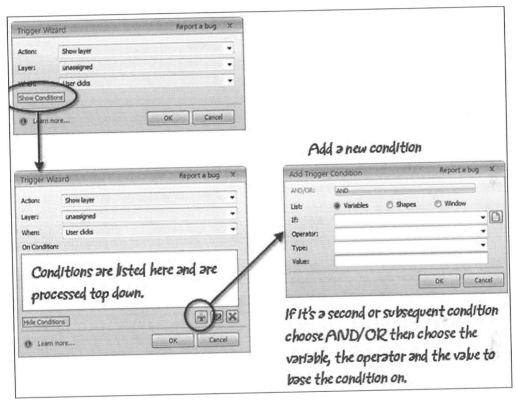

Conditions can be used to restrict or control movement within a course. For example, you may want to ensure that slide 15 is complete, and the **Acknowledge** button is set to a value of true in order to jump to a slide that contains the course completion certificate.

Conditions can also be used to display course progress. For example, there may be an activity where the learner needs to type some comments or they need to complete an exercise before the activity, and the current section of the course is marked as completed.

Conditions become more powerful when used to evaluate variables along with object states or even other variables. For example, you could have a home page with images that represent each section of a course. When the learner reaches the end of a section, a variable is adjusted to indicate the section has been completed and based on that, when the user returns to the home screen, the state of the section image is adjusted to include a checkmark. The learner is restricted from using the **Next** button to proceed until all of the section images have the state of completed.

The order of conditions is important. Conditions are evaluated, like triggers, from the top down.

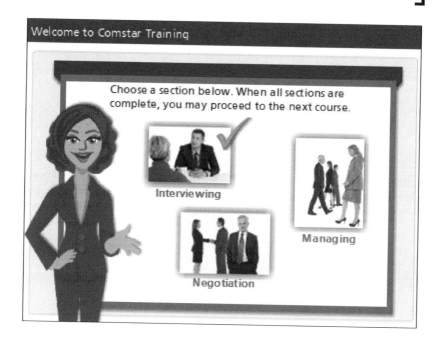

When defining conditions, you can create one or more conditions. When Adding multiple conditions they are joined together using **AND** or **OR** conditions. For example:

- Condition 1: "Jump to the next slide when the media **Sound 1** completes"

  OR

- Condition 2: "when the **Continue** button is visited"

There are three elements that you can apply conditions to; variables, shapes, and the player window/lightboxes.

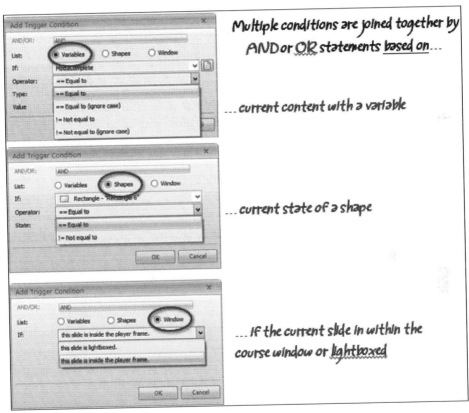

Follow along...

Continuing with `Exercise 6- Sales Training`, this exercise completes the steps needed to add intelligence to the menu so that Storyline keeps track of learner progress while restricting the learner from jumping ahead without completing the three sections of this course.

Part 1 – setting up variables and tracking progress

In the previous exercises you created three variables called Mod1Complete, Mod2Complete, and Mod3Complete. These variables are true/false and each have a default value of false. When the learner completes a section we want these variables to adjust to true. Follow the proceeding steps to do this:

1. Navigate to slide **2.2 Details** and switch to **Normal View**.

2. Add a new trigger that adjusts the variable **Mod1Complete** to true when timeline starts by changing the **Value** drop-down menu to **Value** and, in the box next to this, choosing the value of **True** when **Timeline starts** for **2.2 Details**.

3. Copy this trigger, navigate to slide **3.2 Details**, paste the trigger, and edit it so the variable is **Mod2Complete**.

4. Repeat this for slide **4.2 Details,** switching the variable to **Mod3Complete**.

5. Switch to **Slide Master View** and navigate to the **Menu** layout.

6. Now we'll set up triggers that will evaluate the three completion variables, and adjust the states of the corresponding circles on the menu slide:

    1. Add a new trigger that changes the state of **Oval 1** to the **Completed** state when the **Timeline starts**.

    2. Click on **Show Conditions** then click on the **Add New Condition (+)** button.

    3. From the **IF** drop-down list, select **Mod1Complete**.

    4. From the **Operator** drop-down list, select **==Equal to.**

    5. From the **Type** drop-down list, select **Value.**

    6. From the **Value** drop-down list, select **True.**

    7. Click **OK** twice to return to the slide.

    8. Copy this trigger twice.

7. Edit the respective copies to adjust **Oval 2** and **Oval 3** following the preceding steps. Ensure that you also double-click on the condition and adjust the variable being evaluated so that the variable changes from **Mod1Complete** to **Mod2Complete** and **Mod3Complete**.

8. Return to **Normal View** and save the project.

9. Preview the entire project, viewing each of the **Details** screens and testing to ensure that each section contains a checkmark on the menu screen if the section has been completed.

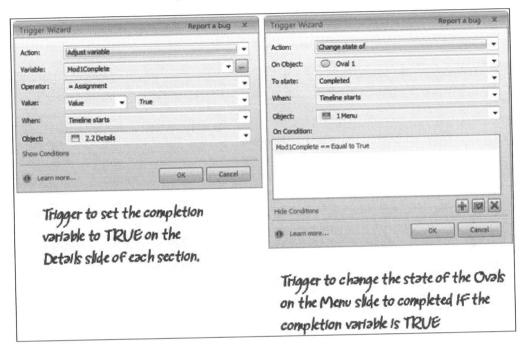

Trigger to set the completion variable to TRUE on the Details slide of each section.

Trigger to change the state of the Ovals on the Menu slide to completed IF the completion variable is TRUE

Part 2 – controlling learner navigation to prevent skipping sections

Now that Storyline knows if a section has been completed, you can limit learner movement, and prevent them from skipping ahead by placing conditions on the **Next** button. Follow the proceeding steps to do this:

1. Switch to **Slide Master View** and choose the **Menu** layout.

2. Add a new trigger that jumps to slide **5.1 You're Done** when the user clicks on the next button.

3. Click on **Show Conditions** and press the **Add Conditions (+)** button.

4. From the **IF** drop-down list, select **Mod1Complete**.

5. From the **Operator** drop-down list, select **=Equal to**.

6. From the **Type** drop-down list, select **Value**.

7. From the **Value** drop-down list, select **True**.

8. Click on **OK.**

9. Click on the **Add Conditions** (+) button, and repeat this for **Mod2Complete** and **Mod3Complete**.

10. Click on **OK** to return to the slide.

11. Switch to **Normal View** and navigate to slide **2.2 Details**. There is a trigger on this slide that controls what happens when the learner clicks on the **Next** button. We want to ensure they are returned to the **Menu** slide if they click on the **Next** button. To do this, locate **Player Triggers** in the **Triggers** panel, and change the trigger so that it jumps to slide **1.2 Menu** when the user clicks on the **Next** button. Repeat this for slide **3.2 Details** and **4.2 Details**.

12. Save the project.

13. Preview the entire project, navigating to each section and attempting to click on the **Next** button from the menu slide to skip to the end. You should not be able to do this until each section is completed.

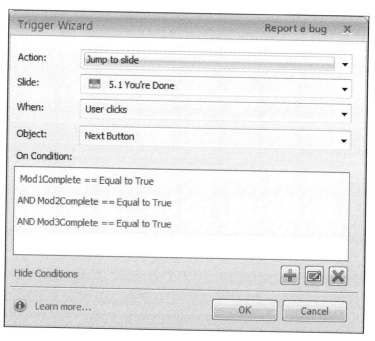

Summary

This chapter introduced powerful methods of customizing and personalizing course content without the complexity of programming!

Key to this was the use of variables to temporarily store information. This information sometimes comes directly from the learner or indirectly based on other conditions.

As you discovered, creating a variable is one thing, and doing something with it, another. This is where triggers and references come in; to create action that enables the display of variable content, or the manipulation of it.

You uncovered methods of refining actions by using conditional logic. Through this you were able to base action on criteria that could be as simple as a single condition, or as complex as multiple conditions that evaluated not only variable content but object states as well.

Storyline provides a tremendous wealth of programming-like possibilities without draining your brain. The trick is to be mindful of the order of events; almost everything in Storyline is processed in a top-down manner, so placing conditions and triggers in a logical sequence is critical to achieving the desired results. It's a good idea to ask yourself "what do I want to do, when do I want to do it?" to help you establish the correct order for your triggers and conditions.

The Articulate community houses a lot of information and examples on all aspects of Storyline, including these interesting examples of using variables:

- `http://community.articulate.com/blogs/jeanette/archive/2013/01/04/using-a-simple-storyline-number-variable-to-show-learners-how-many-objects-they-ve-found.aspx`
- `https://articulate-workshops.s3.amazonaws.com/2012/Storyline-Workshop/storyline-variables.html`
- `http://community.articulate.com/tutorials/products/adding-text-variables.aspx`
- `http://community.articulate.com/tutorials/products/building-a-simple-counter.aspx`

Now that you've worked quite substantially on slide and layer content, let's pop up to the thousand feet view and map out a course, creating paths for the learner to explore from the vantage point of the driver's seat.

7
Creating Learning Paths

As you have seen in previous chapters, interactive e-learning contains activities, and interactions that require learner input, and often provide simple feedback.

Sometimes more complex instruction, where the learner is provided with an opportunity to make a decision, is needed. Based on those decisions, the learner may be provided with feedback, or not, then routed down a specific learning path. This technique is called **branching**.

In this section you learn how to create branched e-learning with Storyline, including:

- Principles of branching
- Controlling presentation order
- Understanding slide properties
- Customizing slide navigation

Principles of branching

Basic branching is present in most e-learning courses and is commonly disguised as navigational choices. In its simplest form, branching helps break away from strictly linear courses to interactive courses where the learner can make a decision of some form.

Examples of navigational branching include menus that present topic choices, areas of interest, or job roles where a learner can decide how they would like to proceed. Depending on their choice, they are taken down one of several available learning paths; as in the following example where the learner can choose the character **Samantha** or **David**, or they can decide to review basic information by clicking on the sticky note instead.

With Storyline, creating this kind of basic branching is straightforward, and you've practiced this with the sales training course created in the previous chapter.

The same techniques can be used for complex branching when the learner needs to make a judgment call, or they have a decision to make as part of a scenario or simulation. As in real life, these choices are rarely as simple as a single multiple choice question. Every decision has consequences. Branching allows you to simulate real world situations and illustrate the effects of these decisions to your learners, giving your courses a high level of realism.

In Storyline this would normally involve concealing player navigation to focus the learner on the situation at hand, and use custom triggers on slide objects to control navigation.

The following example shows an interactive scenario where the learner must review information and form an opinion before the meeting starts. There is a 5 minute countdown timer that creates a sense of urgency, just like in real life. Once the opinion is formed, the learner clicks on **go to meeting** which advances to a slide where they can make their decision, and view the consequences, then continue on with the next scenario.

Complex branching of this kind involves challenges, choices, and consequences. Each decision produces a consequence, with or without feedback, that moves the learner to the next challenge, and so on. Decision-making activities help the learner think through what they would do if the situation were really happening to them, and help them make appropriate decisions.

To develop a course with branching that flows logically, you will want to draw it out, organizing the challenges, choices, and the consequences for each choice. It can become complex when a choice leads to the end of the branch (failure), or if the learner is allowed a second try (looping back). Sometimes using mind map software can help, or just paper and pen, so that you have a plan for which trigger goes where and why that happens as opposed to adhoc while developing (which is infinitely harder and more time consuming).

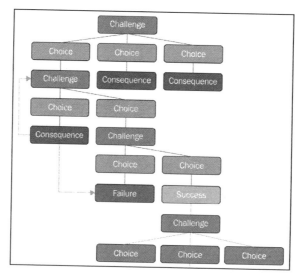

If the story is well written and the situation realistic, the result is a teachable moment when the learner gains a new level of comprehension, and an ability to apply this learning in the real world.

E-learning courses that contain complex branching tend to focus on principles or situations that guide decisions. The real complexity with branching lies in realistic and viable storytelling much more than specific steps undertaken in Storyline.

The majority of e-learning courses don't require complex branching. Sometimes simpler is better particularly for process related topics, or courses that focus on information awareness. All courses can benefit from simple, navigational branching to alleviate boredom from repeatedly clicking on the **Next** button. Letting learners make some decisions along the way will help keep their attention. A note of caution here; if no real decision needs to be made, don't make one up just because you want to include some branching; this will backfire. If the decision is viable and meaningful, use branching to include it as opposed to making the decision on behalf of the learner.

A number of resources are provided at the end of the chapter to support you in writing and developing effective scenario-based and simulation-based e-learning that involves complex branching.

Controlling presentation order

To create branched scenarios or learning that provides choices to the user, we must first take a closer look at the presentation order that Storyline uses presentation order.

By default, slides and scenes follow a linear order. When the learner clicks on the **Next** button they are taken to the next sequential slide or scene. Lines and arrows that appear in Story View indicate the relationship between slides and scenes.

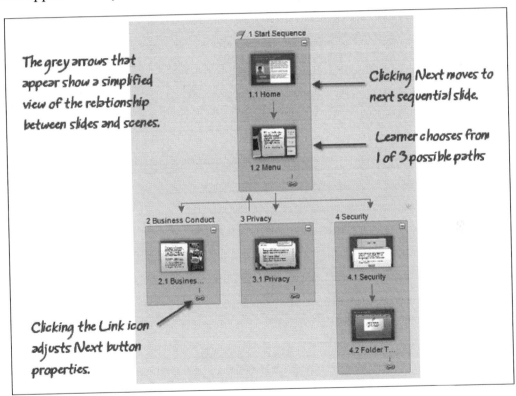

When you select a slide, the detail of slide relationships show as blue arrows between slides. You can click on these arrows to adjust the trigger that defines them.

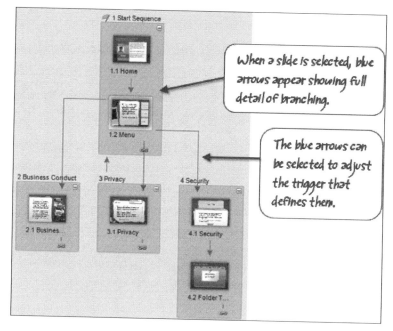

Nonlinear courses use triggers either to customize how the **Next** button behaves, or to customize buttons to jump to particular branches based on learner selection.

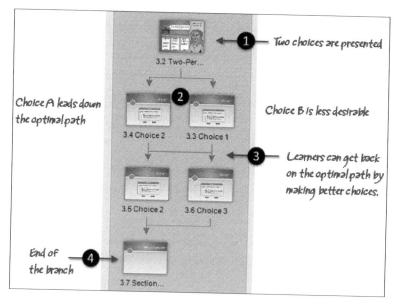

Here's how to adjust the **Next** button:

1. Navigate to the slide where you want to adjust the **Next** button.

2. In the **Triggers** panel, edit the trigger for the **Next** button by clicking on the **next slide** link, and changing this to another slide or scene.

   Or

   Click once on the chain link icon that appears below the slide in Story View, and choose **Link to Slide** or **Link to Scene**.

Here's how to adjust navigational Triggers:

1. In Story View, click on any blue line/arrow that appears between slides or scenes.

2. The **Trigger Wizard** appears. Make any adjustments that are needed and click on **OK** to save the changes. Story View will automatically update to visually reflect any changes made.

Story View doesn't reflect what the learner sees. It provides a big picture map of all course content for visual assistance while you are developing. This view is particularly helpful when there is branching, as you are able to easily identify where branching occurs. Scenes translate into groups in the menu when the course is previewed or published. Also remember that Storyline's automatic slide numbering doesn't affect how the learner proceeds through content when branching is used (that is, the learner may go to slide 3.4 before slide 3.3).

Follow along...

This exercise will expand the content and functionality of the course titled `Exercise 6- Sales Training` created in the previous chapter. In this exercise you will insert a prebuilt two-person scenario slide and will begin to customize it so that a simulated customer call is occurring that presents a challenge, and prompts the learner to respond. The next exercise will expand on this to add consequences.

1. Open `Exercise 6- Sales Training` and navigate to slide **3.1 Intro**.

2. While in Story View, go to **Insert** | **New Slide** from the ribbon.

3. Choose **Templates | Top Interactions** and then go to **Two-Person Scenario** from the list of available templates. Choose **Import into the Current Scene,** and click on **Import**.

4. Update the theme of the new slide to be the same as the others by selecting slide **3.2 Two-Person Scenario**, selecting the **Design** tab, and then right-clicking on the first design theme in the list (green). Choose **Apply to Selected Slides**.

5. Let's create a new Slide Master for the scenario by selecting the **View** tab and choosing **Slide Master**. Select the 2nd Module 2 layout (light blue circle on right side of the slide), and press *Ctrl + D* to duplicate it, and then do the following:

    1. Rename the layout to **Scenario.**

    2. Delete the placeholder that is in the center of the slide.

    3. Move the text placeholder that is on the right side to act as a title at the top of the slide. Change the alignment of the text in this placeholder to left aligned.

6. Return to **Normal View** and change the layout of **3.2 Two-Person Scenario** by right-clicking on the slide, and choose **Layout** then select **Scenario**.

7. Navigate to slide 3.2 and make the following changes to customize content:

    1. Change the title to **Customer Call.**

    2. Remove the **Choice 3** button and text box from the slide.

    3. Delete the **Choice 2** and **Choice 3** layers that appear in the **Layer** panel.

    4. Change the text in the speech bubble for the lady at the desk to be **I would like to speak to someone about widgets (sounding frustrated)**.

    5. Shorten the length of the orange rectangle to fit within the green area of the slide and change the text to read **What should you say?**

    6. Change the text box for **Choice 1** to read **Is there something specific you would like to discuss?**

    7. Change the text box for **Choice 2** to read **Not a problem. One moment please....**

8. Change **Choice 1** and **Choice 2** buttons to **Say This for both**.

9. When the user clicks on the first **Say This** button, Storyline will display the **Choice 1** layer as you can see by the trigger on this button. Edit the layer so it appears as follows:

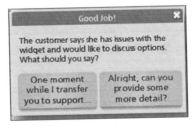

8. Preview slide **3.2 Two-Person Scenario**. Click on the first **Say This** button and notice the pop-up feedback that appears as well as the expression changes on the characters. Click on the **close** button on the pop-up feedback and then close preview.

9. View the **Trigger** panel for this slide and examine the default triggers that are controlling expressions. We won't change this but you should take a moment to make sure you understand why they are there, and what they are doing.

10. Save the file as **Exercise 7- Sales Training**.

Understanding slide properties

Slide properties control how the slide advances, what happens when learners revisit the slide, and player controls that are visible for the slide (the **next** and **previous** buttons).

Viewing slide properties can be done in **Story View** and **Normal View** as shown in the following screenshot:

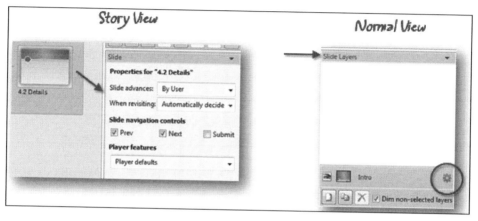

Slide properties are important to understand in order to control slide order and branching behavior. Let's take a closer look at each of the properties that can be adjusted on a per slide basis.

Slide advances

The default is **By User**. This means that the user must click on the **Next** button to advance to the next slide. This can be switched to **Automatically** so that when the timeline ends the next slide is displayed.

When revisiting

This option controls how objects behave when the learner returns to a slide. The default is **Automatically decide** which means if the slide contains objects (graphics, audio, and so on), and no interactivity, Storyline resets the slide to the beginning of the slide's timeline when the learner returns to the slide. If the slide contains interactive elements such as buttons or other objects that include a visited or selected state, Storyline resumes play at the point where the slide was previously left. You can override this by forcing a **Reset to initial state** or **Resume saved state** on a slide-by-slide basis.

For the most part the default of **Automatically decide** works well but there are times when you'll need to override this. Here are two examples:

- A slide plays an audio track while various images and animations appear. When the learner returns, the slide plays this all over again from the beginning. This is what Storyline will do since there is no interactivity. To prevent this, switch the slide properties to **Resume saved state**.

- There is an image on a slide that has two states, normal and a custom state called completed. There are triggers that switch the state to **Completed** after the learner does something. The learner completes what they had to do and the object changes to the completed state which shows a checkmark on the screen. When the learner comes back to the slide, the checkmark is gone. Storyline will reset the slide since the image doesn't have a visited or selected state. To prevent this, change to **Resume saved state**.

Slide navigation controls

By default the player displays native controls including the **Next** and **Previous** buttons for all slides when previewing or viewing a published course. There is also a **Submit** button that appears automatically for slides containing a quiz. You can turn these buttons on or off for each slide.

You may want to turn off these buttons for slides displayed in a lightbox to force the learner to click on the red **x** (close) to close the lightbox. Some courses have these buttons disabled entirely, opting for custom controls on the master slides to create a unique playback experience.

Player features

This option is an extension of slide navigation controls. By selecting **Custom for the selected slide**, you can turn on or off other player controls that appear in the player interface such as the menu, resources, glossary, notes, and the seek bar.

When creating triggers to branch to slides, be sure that you specify the exact slide you want to jump to. If slide order changes later, the link will remain in place using this method, as opposed to generic links to the next or previous slide which can change if the story structure is changed.

Follow along...

Continuing with `Exercise 7- Sales Training` let's now insert slides to create branching for the consequences of the choices the learner makes.

1. Insert a **New Slide** after slide 3.2 using the **Scenario** layout and change the name and title on the slide to **Support Team**. This slide will contain the response when the learner decides to forward the call to technical support. Make the following changes to this slide:

    1. Using *Ctrl* + click, copy the woman at the desk and speech bubble, and the female character with headset from slide 3.2, and paste this into the new **Support Team** slide.

    2. Right-click the female character and change this character to **Male 1**.

    3. Duplicate the speech bubble, reposition, and edit as shown in the following screenshot.

    4. Move and enlarge the woman at the desk to the lower left corner of the screen, and adjust the size and content of the speech bubble as shown in the following screenshot.

    5. Insert a new button; format it to red with the text **You have failed. Click to try again**.

    6. Change the trigger on the new button so that it jumps to slide 3.2 when clicked.

2. Navigate to the slide **3.2 Two-Person Scenario** and change the second **Say This** button to jump to the new **Support Team** slide just created.

3. Click on the **Choice 1** layer and adjust the trigger for the **One moment...** button so that it also jumps to slide **3.3 Support Team** when clicked.

4. Save the file.

5. Duplicate **3.3 Support Team** twice renaming the first copy to be **Reception** and the second to **Sales Team**.

6. Select **3.4 Reception** and make the following adjustments:

    1. Change the title to **Reception.**

    2. Change the customer speech bubble to **Sure! The widget is a bit wonky but I need two more**.

    3. Right-click on the male character and change this to **Female 1**.

    4. Change the Female 1 speech bubble to **No problem. Let me transfer you to Sales**.

    5. Change the button to green and the text in the button to **Good job! Click to go to Sales.**

    6. Change the trigger on the button to jump to slide **3.5 Sales Team**.

7. Select slide 3.2, click on the **Choice 1** layer and change the trigger for the second button that starts with **Alright, can you....**so that it jumps to slide **3.4 Reception** when clicked.

8. Save the file.

9. Select slide **3.5 Sales Team** and make the following changes:

    1. Change the title to **Sales Team**

    2. Change the customer speech bubble to **I'd like to order two widgets.**

    3. Change the male character to **Female 6** and edit the speech bubble to be **This is Sales, how may we help?**

    4. Change the button to orange and text to **Click to continue.**

    5. Adjust the trigger on the button so that it jumps to slide **3.6 Details** when clicked.

10. Select slide **3.6 Details**, rename the slide, and change the title to **Summary**.

11. Switch to **Story View**. Here you will see how the branching you just created flows from slide-to-slide. We have stopped branching after the first conversation but conceivably this could continue on with the sales team, then responding to the customer, and so on.

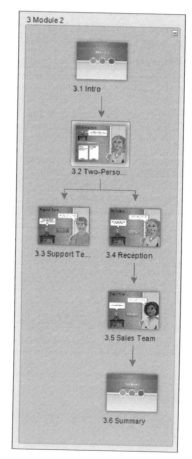

12. Preview the scene. Test all the ways that you can work through the scenario, both right and wrong. You may notice upon making an incorrect choice, you are return to slide 3.2 but other buttons have changed color (state), or the **Choice 1** layer is visible. This behavior is a default in Storyline and we'll take a look at how to correct this next. For now, let's save the file.

Customizing slide navigation

Once you have course content organized and navigation, including branching, in place you may want to take a closer look at how the slide appears to the learner.

As mentioned earlier, you can work with slide properties to configure what player controls are visible for a particular slide, or group of slides. This feature comes in handy when you have a course that contains a scenario or simulation where you want the learner to interact with what is on the slide, and not be distracted by other player controls.

To create a seamless experience, you can turn off player controls for certain sections of a course, and use custom controls instead.

In the following example, the learner must explore the scene, clicking on the various objects to uncover issues. Once all issues have been uncovered, a custom button appears in the lower right corner prompting the learner to proceed. Notice that the menu on the left isn't visible, nor are the next and previous buttons at the bottom.

Follow along...

This exercise will continue with `Exercise 7- Sales Training` to touch up the way the learner views the scenario:

1. Switch to Story View and click on the **3.2 Two-Person Scenario** slide.

2. To ensure that this slide doesn't show previous responses when the learner returns to it, adjust the slide properties so that when revisiting it is set to **Reset to initial state**.

3. Let's customize the player so that some of the player controls are hidden while the learner interacts with the scenario, to do this follow these steps:

    1. Use *Ctrl* + click to select slides 3.2, 3.3, 3.4, and 3.5.

    2. In the slide properties panel, uncheck the **Previous** and **Next** buttons to hide the display of each.

    3. Also in slide properties, in the **Player Features** drop-down menu, go to **Custom for the selected slides**.

    4. Be sure that the only item checked is **Resources**.

4. Save the file.

5. Preview the scene. Notice how the player controls appear at the beginning, disappear during the scenario, and reappear at the end of the scene.

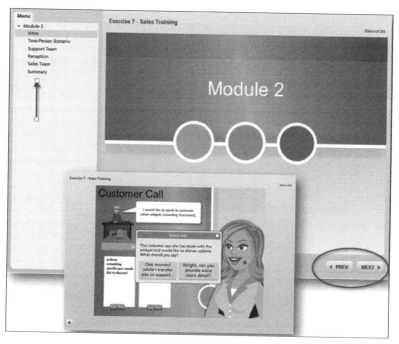

Summary

Branching opens up a world of possibilities that can assist in transforming typical, linear e-learning to a whole new level of interactivity.

The most complex part of branching doesn't happen within Storyline, it happens on paper; the process of determining how the story will unfold and upfront planning needed to bring the story to life anticipating decision points, and determining consequences in a logical and realistic way.

There are many storytelling resources on the internet that will help improve your storytelling skills, and help you work through the planning stages.

Here are a few resources that will help you get a head start:

- Storytelling (not e-learning specific but informative) `http://en.wikipedia.org/wiki/Storytelling`
- Collection of storytelling articles `http://www.dmoz.org/Arts/Performing_Arts/Storytelling`
- Books `http://www.amazon.com/mn/search/?_encoding=UTF8&camp=1789&creative=390957&field-keywords=how%20to%20tell%20stories&linkCode=ur2&sprefix=how%20to%20tell%20s,stripbooks,302&tag=therapeleablo-20&url=search-alias%3Dstripbooks`
- The Articulate Rapid Elearning Blog `http://www.articulate.com/rapid-elearning/an-easy-way-to-build-branched-scenarios-for-e-learning/`
- Multimedia e-Learning `http://multimedialearning.com/creating-rapid-e-learning-scenarios/`
- Suddenly Smart branching examples (with great storylines) `http://www.suddenlysmart.com/examples.htm`
- Patti Shank via eLearning Guild `http://www.learningsolutionsmag.com/articles/887/beginning-instructional-authoring-getting-good-scenario-content-from-smes`
- Cathy Moore branching scenario example `http://blog.cathy-moore.com/2010/05/elearning-example-branching-scenario/`

- Cathy Moore action mapping
  `http://blog.cathy-moore.com/2012/01/how-action-mapping-can-change-your-design-process/`
- Ray Jimenez, advice and examples of stories and scenarios for elearning
  `http://vignettestraining.blogspot.ca/`

Simple branching is used all the time and is a great way to involve learners. Complex branching is less common and works best when a realistic walk-through of simulated events is used to engage the learner, and to educate. Before planning a complex branched scenario, be sure that you have support from, and direct access to, subject matter experts that will help to make the story realistic, accurate, and helpful; without their support, creating meaningful scenarios with branching will prove challenging.

Branching is one method used to test comprehension through the decision-making process as events unfold. Another simpler way is by inserting quiz questions into your content and this will be the focus of the next chapter.

8
Testing Learner Knowledge

Most e-learning courses include some form of testing as a method of assessing a learner's level of understanding and to provide support and feedback during the learning process.

Traditionally this takes the form of a quiz at the end of a section or the end of a course. With Storyline, you're not restricted to grouping all of your quiz questions together. You can choose to add one or more questions, when and where it makes sense to provide the learner an opportunity to assess their understanding.

In this chapter you will learn about:

- The categories and types of prebuilt questions in Storyline
- Creating, editing, and customizing questions
- Adjusting the look and feel of questions and feedback
- Converting static content into interactive quizzes
- Displaying and customizing feedback, scores, and results

Question categories and types

There are over 20 types of questions that you can create in Storyline. Questions are organized into three categories:

- **Graded**: Predefined questions to test learner knowledge that require a response (right or wrong) with corresponding feedback, and which can be scored
- **Survey**: Predefined questions to collect information that don't have right or wrong answers and are not scored
- **Freeform**: Custom-built questions that are created from the slide's content

Each question category offers a number of question types. We'll focus on graded and survey questions first. Here is a snapshot of the types of questions available in Storyline:

- **Graded question types**:

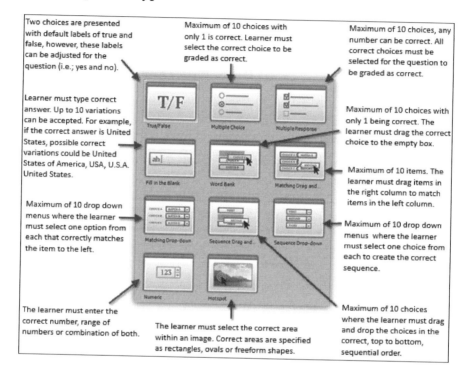

- **Survey question types:**

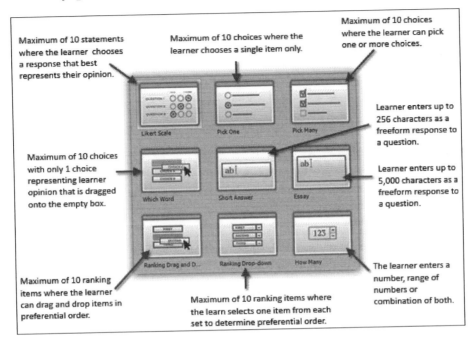

Creating, editing, and customizing questions

This topic walks through the basics of adding quizzes to your e-learning courses. You will be creating a new project file that will include a variety of quiz questions with scoring and results.

Creating graded or survey questions

New questions are created in Storyline by inserting a quiz slide.

1. From the **Home** or **Insert** tab, select **New Slide**.
2. From the **Insert Slides** window, select the **Quizzing** tab.
3. Choose the **Graded** or **Survey** category tab along the top of the window.
4. Select a question type thumbnail and click on the **Insert** button.

Initial setup of graded or survey questions

After inserting a new question slide, **Form View** of the question editor automatically opens. This will look familiar to you if you have used Articulate Quizmaker before. From here you can:

*   Enter question text
*   Enter answer choices
*   Specify the correct answer
*   Control how feedback is given
*   Allocate points for each question

Follow along...

The project that you will create in this chapter is a security-related quiz that will consist of an instructional page, four quiz questions, and a results slide. You will be using built-in Storyline templates to construct this quiz.

1. Create a new project and choose **Insert | New Slide**, select the **Template** tab and then choose **Character Display Panels** from the template drop-down menu along the top.
2. Double-click on **Anchor Desk** to insert this into the current scene.
3. Enter the title `Identity Theft` at the top of the slide and rename the slide **Instructions**.
4. Enter the following instructions where it says **click to add text**:
    *   Pam is about to have her identity stolen!
    *   By answering the following questions correctly, you can help her regain her identity.
    *   Click on Pam to get started.

5. Delete the first blank slide.

6. From the **Insert** menu, insert an illustrated character and choose **Female 20**. Crop the character so that only the head and shoulders appear. Resize to make the character larger and place in the bottom middle of the slide beneath the instructions.

7. Create the following new states for the character:

    ○ **Normal**: As it is

    ○ **Hover**: Change to happy expression

    ○ **Reveal Eyebrows**: Crop the image from the bottom so that only the eyebrows and upper section of the image appear in this state

    ○ **Reveal Eyes**: copy from the bottom so that only the eyes and upper section of the image appear

    ○ **Reveal Chin**: Crop so that only the section above the chin appears

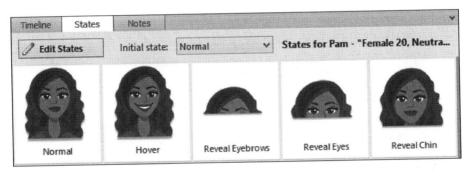

8. In the Timeline, change the name of the character object to Pam.

9. Save the file as Exercise 8 – Identity Theft.

10. Insert a new slide, choose the **Quizzing** tab and select the graded question type of **True/False**.

11. In the Question Editor, enter the following question text, setting **False** as the correct choice:

    Her driver's license has vanished. She should call the police.

12. Save and close out of the question editor to return to the Normal View.

13. Right-click on the second slide thumbnail in the **Scene List** and change the **Layout** to **Title Only** from the **Layout** selections. If the question does not appear to have the correct formatting, you can right-click on the slide again and choose **Reset**.

14. Copy the **Pam** character from the first slide, switch to Master Slides, navigate to the **Title Only** slide layout and paste the character into the slide. Move the character to the upper-right corner.

15. Duplicate the character. Rename the original copy **Pam no ID**. Right-click on the image and format the picture so that brightness and contrast are set to **-100%** and the shape fill is a solid, dark red.

16. Place the duplicated copy on top and align the two images. Later in this chapter, you will add triggers that control the expression and visibility of this character depending on the answers a learner selects during the quiz.

17. Switch back to the **Normal** view, navigate to the first slide and add a trigger to the **Pam** character so that it jumps to the next slide when clicked.

18. Switch over to the second slide and add **Pam's identity has been stolen!**, in bold, red letters beneath the image of Pam. In the Timeline, adjust the timing so that the question text and the **True/False** responses start at the 1.5 second mark.

19. Save the file and preview the scene.

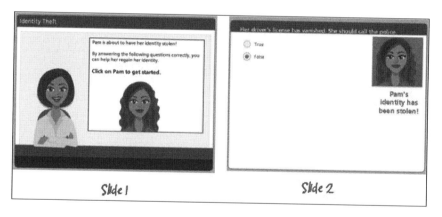

Configuring graded or survey questions

There are several options that can help you configure the behavior of each question. This is done from the ribbon in the **Question Editor**. To open the question editor, click on the **Edit** button in the **Question** panel on the right side of the window.

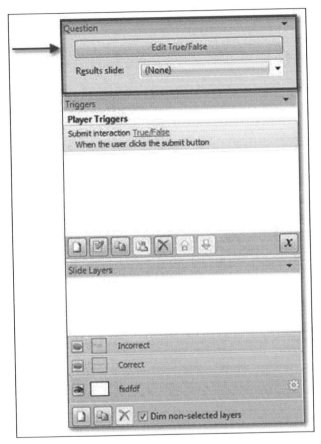

The question editor is divided into several sections. To configure a question, you'll choose options from the **Display** and **Scoring** segments. Some formatting options also appear in the **Clipboard**, **Text**, and **Insert** sections of the ribbon as shown in the following screenshot:

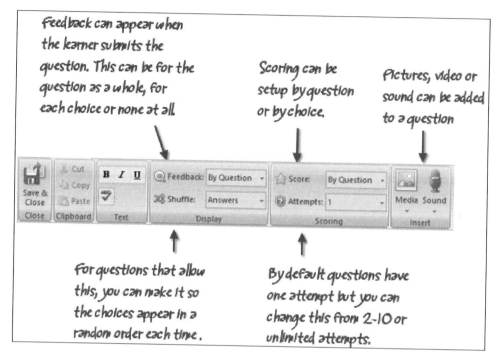

Let's take a moment to review some key points regarding question configuration:

- **Display**:
  - **Feedback**: For graded questions, you can set up one incorrect and one correct message for a question which is then displayed once the learner submits his/her choice. Alternatively, some question types allow you to set up a message for each choice in a question. This is a great way to add a touch of customization to your quizzes by provided context sensitive feedback based on learner's choice. For survey questions, you can set up just one message regardless of the choice the learner makes.

By default, Storyline will move to the next slide when a question is completed. You can control this by clicking on the **More** button within the **Feedback** area in the question editor. From here, you can add some formatting to the feedback text, include a sound file, and choose which slide to branch to. For example, you have a 10 question quiz. The learner must complete the whole quiz unless they answer question 7 correctly, in that case, they can jump to the end. You would set up branching for that question so the correct response jumps to a slide that follows the quiz.

- **Shuffle**: This is a good option to enable as a way to prevent potential cheating by using a new random order each time a question is viewed. Keep in mind that matching and sequence question types automatically shuffle the choices, so the **Shuffle** option appears disabled. Also keep in mind that you shouldn't shuffle questions that have an **All of the above** choice.

- **Required**: This appears only for survey questions to determine if a learner can skip a question or if it must be answered.

- **Scoring**:

  - **Score**: This applies to graded questions and can be set up by a question where you assign a point value for a correct answer and another point value for an incorrect answer. Alternatively, for some question types, you can set up a point value for each option. This is often termed as a **weighted quiz** that tallies up your score based on the choices you make for each question asked (that is, question 1 has three choices where choice *a* is 4 points, choice *b* is 2, choice *c* is 0).

  - **Attempts**: This gives learners extra attempts to get a question correct. Once the learner has used up the specified number of attempts without getting the correct answer, the question will be scored as incorrect.

  - **Submit**: When working with hotspot question types, there will be additional options to determine when a question is scored: when the learner clicks on the **Submit** button or when they click, double-click, or right-click anywhere on the slide.

- **Insert**:

  - **Media**: A picture, video, or sound file can be added to a question through the options here or you can add media to a question using Slide View instead. You can also add narration to question or choice feedback.

Question feedback

When you configure a question to include feedback, whether by question or by choice, a new layer in the question slide is created and it contains the feedback. The layers created are named *incorrect*, *correct*, and *try again* for question-level feedback and are given the name of the question choices for choice-level feedback.

The look and feel of a question slide is controlled by Slide Masters, however the look and feel of feedback layers in a question slide is controlled by **Feedback Masters**. The Feedback Master operates just like Slide Masters and is dedicated to controlling the formatting of question feedback and slide layers.

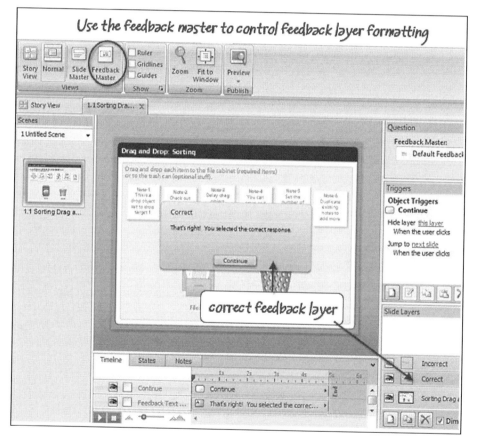

Feedback layers operate in the same fashion as other layers do and can be completely customized by adding and formatting text, media, animations, transitions, and so on.

Follow along...

The following exercise is a continuation of the previous section that will incorporate additional questions, feedback, and triggers. Be sure to have Exercise 8 – Identity Theft open.

1. While positioned on the second slide, insert a new graded quiz question. This time, select **Multiple Choice** as the format.

2. Set up the question as follows:
   - **Question**: What does identity theft refer to?
   - **Choice 1**: Stolen government documents
   - **Choice 2**: Stolen name badges
   - **Choice 3**: Online financial account access
   - **Choice 4**: All of the above

3. Set Choice 4 as the correct answer and make sure that the answers do not shuffle. Save and close to return to Normal View.

4. Change the layout of this slide to be **Title Only** as you did with the second slide.

5. Choose **View | Feedback Master** and move the elements that are on the master slide to appear near the bottom of the slide. Repeat this by selecting all objects on each layout and moving those to appear properly within the grey box at the bottom of the slide.

6. Change the grey box on the master slide to a variation of blue.

7. Switch back to Normal View.

 Notice this slide and the previous one have correct and incorrect layers. These are placed in by default. You can click on each layer to see how the changes you just made in the Feedback Master apply. You can edit feedback for this question through the layers or by selecting **Edit** and using the question editor to do this. Editing directly through layers allows more flexibility in terms of adjusting look and feel and incorporating other objects.

8. Save and then preview the scene to see the incorrect and correct feedback in action.

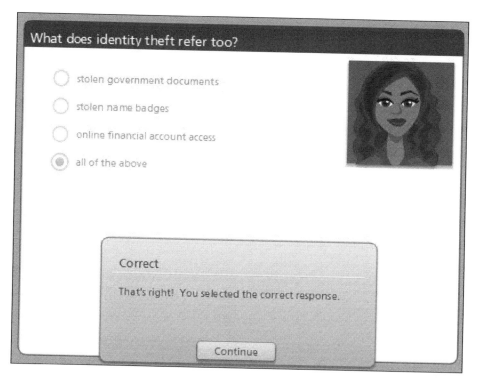

Scoring, results, and review

As you have seen, graded questions and question choices can be assigned a point value in the question editor. When the learner submits a question, the point value is adjusted.

If you want to show learners how they have performed on any combination of questions, you can do that by inserting a **result slide** into the story. You need to identify which questions you want to use for calculating the results and then insert the result slide anywhere in the course. You can insert more than one result slide in a course.

Inserting a result slide

You can insert a result slide by following these steps:

1. From the **Home** or **Insert** tab, select **New Slide**.

2. From the **Insert Slides** window, select the **Quizzing** tab.

3. Choose the **Result Slides** tab along the top of the window.

4. Select a result type thumbnail and click on the **Insert** button.

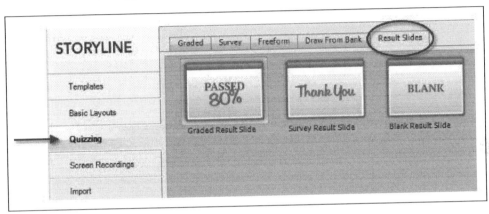

 The blank result slide is most often used when you want to create a custom slide that looks and functions in a specific way. You can build the slide you need and then insert quiz variables to display results.

After selecting a result slide type, the **Result Slide Properties** window automatically appears. Here you can determine which questions to use in the result slide, passing score, and timer to set the maximum allowable time to complete the question(s) included in this result slide.

There are also a number of options you can select to customize what is included on a result slide. You can further customize the layout and object formatting of the slide as you would a regular slide.

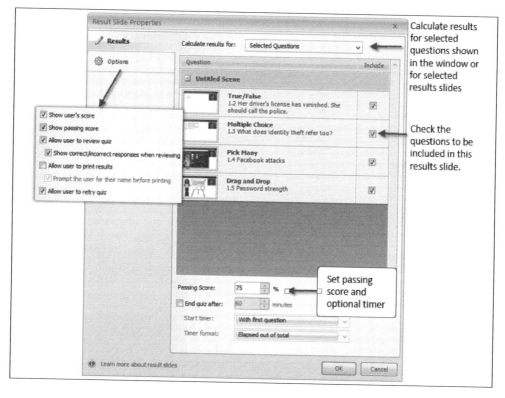

After configuring a result slide and clicking on **OK** at the bottom of the **Result Slide Properties** window, a new slide will be inserted into your project. A sample of a result slide as seen in Slide View is shown in the following screenshot. Depending on the options selected, one or more variable placeholders will appear in the center of the slide with one or more blue buttons along the bottom.

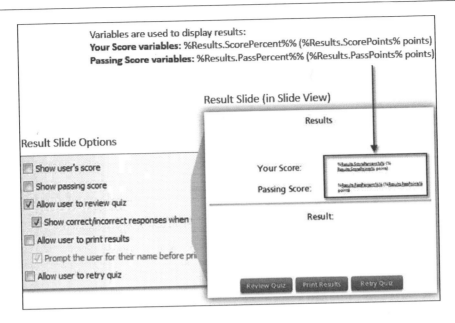

The result slide includes two additional layers, one for a success message and the other for a failure message. These messages apply to the feedback the learner receives upon completing all of the questions included in a specific results page (individual question feedback and question choice feedback remain intact).

Unlike question feedback layers, the success and failure layers are not controlled by a Feedback Master. You can apply other Slide Master layouts to the result slide and can format result slide objects and layers using regular formatting commands.

Here is an example of a published quiz where the result slide indicates the learner has passed the quiz:

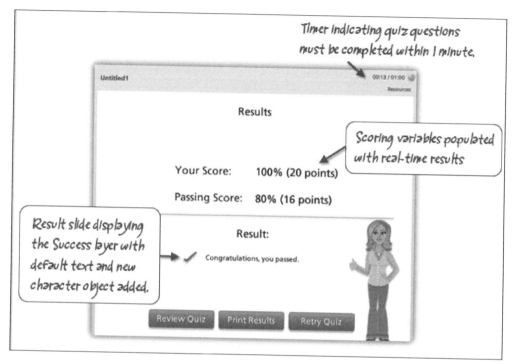

 You can use multiple results' slides in a course, but only one result slide can be tracked in an LMS. You can combine scores from multiple results' slides to create a final result slide with a consolidated score.

Customizing feedback further

The result slide options allow you to include a post-quiz review and a retry button. The retry button lets the learner retake the quiz from the beginning, updating previously recorded scores with the latest attempt.

The post-quiz review option lets the learner go back through each question noting the correct answers for each question. By default, Storyline indicates if the learner got the question right or wrong with an indicator at the bottom of the question slide.

You can customize the post-review feedback to add specific comments by first making sure the **Allow user to review quiz** option is selected in the result slide options, then following the steps below to customize the feedback.

1. Navigate to the question you wish to add post-quiz feedback to and select the **Edit** button in the **Question** panel on the right side of the Storyline workspace.

2. At the bottom of the window there is a **Post-quiz Feedback** option, type some initial text into this field.

3. Click on **Save and Close** to return to Normal View.

4. A new layer called **Review** now appears in the question slide. Edit this layer as needed to customize the wording, look, and feel.

 You can edit the layout so that review formatting is consistent for all questions by editing the **Review** layout in the Feedback Master.

5. Repeat for each question that you would like to include customized feedback for, otherwise the default will indicate correct or incorrect only.

 You can hide the additional review layer content you may have set up for a question if the learner answers the question correctly. You can do this by placing a trigger on the review layer of the question slide that hides the layer if the correct option (shape) has the state of selected. The green correct banner will still appear along the bottom during the review, but the additional content you may have created will not appear. You can also adjust the retry quiz button so it only displays if the quiz was failed by moving the retry quiz button to the failure layer in the result slide.

Follow along...

This exercise is a continuation of the previous exercise. You will create two new slides and prepare them to be converted to interactive quiz questions.

1. Insert a new slide at the end of the story using the **Character Display Panels** template and the **Chalkboard** layout. Rename this slide to `Facebook attacks`.

2. Change the layout of this slide to **Title Only**.

3. Enter the title as `What are the most common types of malicious attacks on Facebook?`.

4. Move the chalkboard image to the left side of the slide and shrink its width so that it is not covering up all of the character that appears on the right side.

5. Insert three different illustrated characters onto the chalkboard, it doesn't matter which ones but make each quite small. In the Timeline, name the character objects as `Character A`, `Character B`, and `Character C`.

6. Insert three textboxes beside each character as follows: viral infection, identity theft, and bullying. Change the corresponding characters and expressions as you see fit to express each of those titles.

7. Save the file.

8. Insert a new slide at the end of the story using the **Character Display Panels** template and the **Flipchart 2** layout. Rename this slide to `Password strength`.

9. Change the title in the slide to be `How strong do you think Pam's password is?`.

10. Move the character, flipchart, and text placeholder over to the left side of the slide. Stretch out the flipchart and the text holder, then type the following text into the text placeholder:

    Most people, including Pam, have a lot of passwords. Pam often uses her mother's maiden name. How strong do you think this password is?

11. Change the character to be **Pam** (Female 20).

12. Change the slide layout to be **Title Only**.

13. Insert a rectangle for the character to hold. Name the object **Password** in the Timeline and then perform the following steps:

    1. Add the following text in the rectangle:

       Mother's maiden name

    2. Size the text down, make the rectangle small about 70 x 70 and adjust the margins of the textbox, if needed, to make the text fit.

    3. Use **Shape Fill** and using the color picker tool fill with a yellow color that matches the existing yellow papers the character is holding.

    4. Remove the outline and add shadow all around.

14. Copy the newly inserted rectangle, name it strong in the Timeline, and position it on the bottom left of the flipchart. Delete the text, fill with white color, add a green dashed outline, and create a drag over state with a green glow for the rectangle.

15. Copy this rectangle twice, naming the first copy medium and the second weak in the Timeline. Place the copies along the bottom of the flipchart and then perform the following steps:

    1. Adjust the middle instance to have an orange dashed border and orange glow for the drag over state.

    2. Adjust the right instance to have a red dashed border and a red glow for the drag over state.

16. Insert three textboxes, placing each beneath the rectangles with the words strong, medium, and weak respectively.

17. Select the original yellow rectangle that the character is holding and add a drop correct state with a checkmark inserted and drop incorrect state with an X.

18. The last two slides will become interactive questions in the next exercise. For now, save the file and continue onto the next topic.

Converting static content

Storyline has a unique feature that allows you to take a regular slide with images, text, and other objects, and convert it to a quiz question. This creates a **freeform question** and lets you transform the existing static content into interactive content. This is also the option you'd use to create a question from scratch when you don't want to use the pre-built graded or survey question types.

Freeform question types

There are five types of freeform questions available:

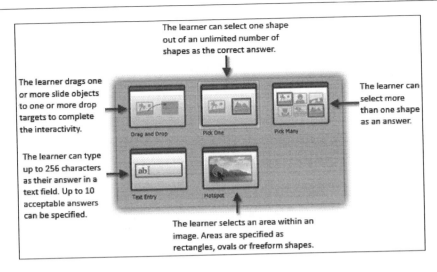

The learner can select one shape out of an unlimited number of shapes as the correct answer.

The learner drags one or more slide objects to one or more drop targets to complete the interactivity.

The learner can select more than one shape as an answer.

The learner can type up to 256 characters as their answer in a text field. Up to 10 acceptable answers can be specified.

The learner selects an area within an image. Areas are specified as rectangles, ovals or freeform shapes.

You can create a freeform question by navigating to **Insert | New Slide** and selecting the **Freeform** tab, or you can click on the **Convert to Freeform** button while viewing a slide you wish to convert to a freeform question.

In both cases, the slide needs to contain at least 2 images, textboxes, shapes, buttons, hotspots, checkboxes, or radio buttons in order to begin configuring the question. You will also need to add any instructions and quiz question text manually on the slide as this is not entered using the freeform question editor. You would then click on the **Edit** button from the **Questions** panel to configure the question.

 When you designate an object as a question element, a new *selected* state is automatically created for the object. You can use the **Edit States** option to format the selected state accordingly.

Pick One, Pick Many, and Text Entry

These question types are similar to graded and survey questions. **Pick One** is like Multiple Choice and **Pick Many** is like Multiple Response. The difference with the freeform variation is that you can use images as items to select, instead of words only.

Text Entry and hotspot

Text Entry questions operate in the same way for graded, survey, and freeform as do hotspot questions. They appear as freeform options to make it easier to add them to slides with existing content.

Both Text Entry and hotspot questions can be configured for use in a quiz with scoring and feedback, or they can be configured as interactive objects for purposes outside of quizzing. Take a look at the examples of using these two question formats outside of a quiz.

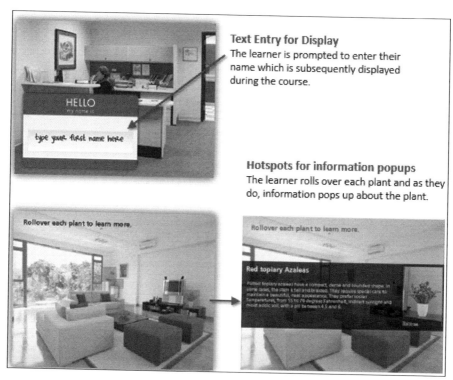

Text Entry for Display
The learner is prompted to enter their name which is subsequently displayed during the course.

Hotspots for information popups
The learner rolls over each plant and as they do, information pops up about the plant.

Don't autofit the **Text Entry** placeholder, otherwise the display may become very tiny if the learner enters a lot of text. Instead, using the **Format** option, choose the **Text Box** tab, select **Do not Autofit** and resize the Text Entry box to be larger.

Drag-and-drop

One of the most exciting features of Storyline is the ability to convert slide objects into drag-and-drop activities. Typically, drag-and-drop is used as a quizzing technique, but you're not limited to that—almost any object can be dragged and dropped with any kind of feedback or action occurring during that process.

The following examples show two radically different uses for drag-and-drop; one is an example of a quiz question and the other is an example of objects that can be dragged-and-dropped on something to display information without using quizzing elements like scoring or feedback:

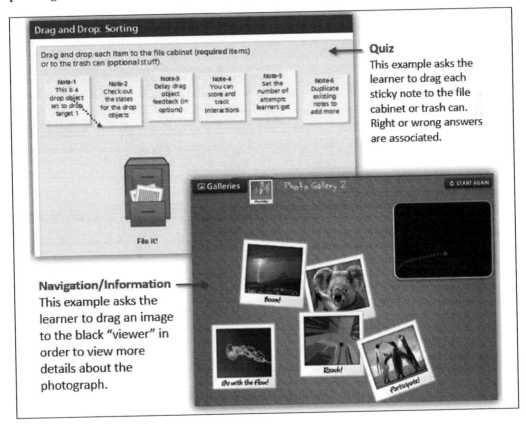

Quiz

This example asks the learner to drag each sticky note to the file cabinet or trash can. Right or wrong answers are associated.

Navigation/Information

This example asks the learner to drag an image to the black "viewer" in order to view more details about the photograph.

Shortcut key

This is a sixth type of freeform question that can only be accessed using the **Convert to Freeform** option. This question type lets a learner answer the question by pressing a key or combination of keys on the keyboard. An example would be this question, "You use the *Ctrl + C* quick key to copy elements but what is the quick key to paste?". When the learner presses *Ctrl + V* on the keyboard, they will see correct feedback.

Keep in mind that Freeform question types are particularly powerful outside of quizzing and can be used to easily add a level of interactivity to content that would normally be static.

Follow along...

This exercise is a continuation of the previous exercise. You'll convert two static slides into interactive content, add a result page, and create triggers to dynamically change the Pam character (revealing more of her identity) with each question that is correctly answered.

1. Navigate to the slide **1.4 Facebook attacks**, switch to Normal View, and choose **Convert to Freeform** from the **Insert** tab. Double-click on the **Pick Many** option.

2. The question editor automatically appears, prompting you to select objects on the slide as items to choose from for this question. Click on the choice A and select **Character A**, choice B is **Character B**, and choice C is **Character C**.

3. Mark choices B and C as correct and then click on **Save and Close**.

4. Navigate to the slide **1.5 Password strength** and choose **Convert to Freeform**. This time, double-click on **Drag and Drop**. In the question editor, do the following:

    1. Check the return item to start point if dropped outside.
    2. Select the **Password** object as the **Drag Item**.
    3. Select the **Weak** rectangle as the correct **Drop Target**.
    4. On the line below, select the **Medium** rectangle as a **Drop Target**.
    5. On the line below that, do the same for the **Strong** rectangle.

5. Save the file and then preview the scene and review all of the questions.

6. Now let's add a result slide to show quiz scores to the learner. To do this, choose **Insert | New Slide** and under **Quizzing**, select the **Result Slides** tab. Double-click on **Graded Results Slide** to insert this at the end of the story.

7. Adjust the result's slide so that the passing grade is **75%** and under **Options**, check the box to allow users to retry the quiz. Click on **OK** to insert the result slide.

8. Change the layout to **Title Only** and add the title to `Your Results!` and then move the text and quiz score variable placeholders so that they are not overtop of the Pam character.

9. Go ahead and save. Then preview this scene answering some questions right and some wrong, to see how the result slide looks.

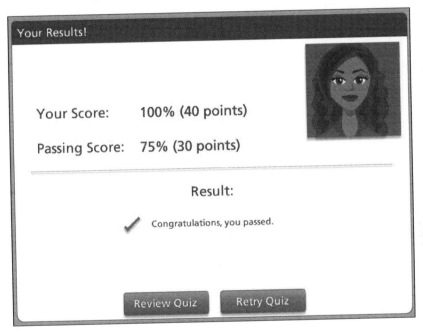

Customizing your quiz

You can add buttons, checkboxes, radio buttons, hotspots, and data entry to any slide. Turn just about any object into a drag-and-drop, add triggers to control quizzing, and customize feedback layers and branching.

Did you notice when you look at the result slide if it has a Success and a Failure layer? You can edit these messages directly within the layer similar to incorrect and correct question feedback.

Follow along...

As the final step in the exercise for this chapter, the Pam character on the master slide is going to be revealed a bit at a time as the learner answers questions correctly. This will be done by leveraging quiz results' variables to add logic so the character state changes based on the current quiz score. To do this, perform the following steps:

1. Switch to **Master Slides** and navigate to the **Title Only** layout.

2. In the **Triggers** panel, click on the **New Trigger** button and create a trigger with the following specifications (be sure to select the **Pam** and not the **Pam no ID** character):

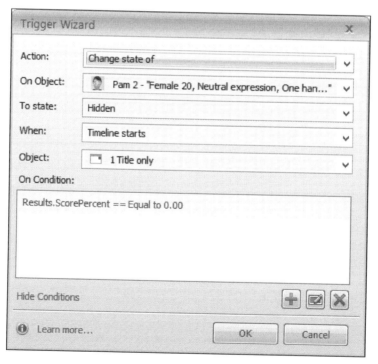

3. In the **Triggers** panel, copy this new trigger four times making the following adjustments to each of the copies:

    1. Change the state to **Reveal Eyebrows** when the **Title Only** timeline starts if **Results.ScorePercent** is set to **25**.

    2. Change the state to **Reveal Eyes** when the **Title Only** timeline starts if **Results.ScorePercent** is set to **50**.

    3. Change the state to **Reveal Chin** when the **Title Only** timeline starts if **Results.ScorePercent** is set to **75**.

    4. Change the state to **Normal** when the **Title Only** timeline starts if **Results.ScorePercent** is set to **100**.

4. Return to Normal View, save and preview the scene.

> Once you create a result slide, you can use quizzing variables to add custom triggers anywhere within a story. The variables are preceded by the name Results and a number if there is more than one result slide in a story. For example, the first result slide variables are Results.ScorePercent, Results.ScorePoints (the score the learner has achieved), Results.PassPercent, and Results.PassPoints (what is required to pass the quiz). The second would be Results1.ScorePercent, the third Result2.ScorePercent, and so on.

5. You can further customize questions and the result slide by editing the feedback messages in the slide layers. We'll do that now with the result slide:

    ○ The **Success** layer: Change the text to read:

      Congratulations, you've helped Pam regain her identity! You scored 75% or better so consider yourself a security expert!

    ○ The **Failure** layer: Change the text to read:

      Unfortunately Pam is still without her identity. If you scored below 25% you should consider stepping away from the computer or perhaps you would like to try the quiz again?

6. Back on the **Your Results!** slide base layer, adjust the quiz variable placeholder that appears in the center of the screen in small text so that only the percentage is shown, not points. You can do this by deleting the `%Results.ScorePoints%` and `%Results.ScorePass%` from each textbox.

7. For this quiz, the **Retry Quiz** button should only appear if the learner fails the quiz. To do this, cut the button out of the result slide base layer and paste it into the **Failure** layer.

8. **Save** and **Preview** the story.

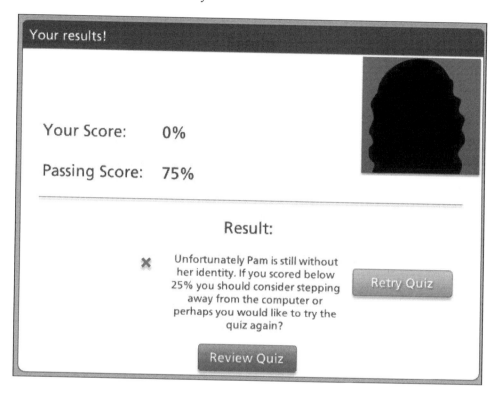

Summary

As you have seen, Storyline offers a great deal of flexibility when creating knowledge checks for your learners. You can deviate from the traditional approach and create highly interactive and frequent checks throughout your material.

Storyline includes a wide variety of pre-built question formats that you can customize easily using all the standard slide editing techniques you already know how to use. You can also create branching scenarios just by redirecting which slide Storyline should go to if the learner answers the question right or wrong.

Outside of the pre-built questions, you've seen that almost any slide can be converted into a quiz with buttons, checkboxes, radio buttons, hotspots, and data entry. And almost any object can be transformed into something that can be dragged-and-dropped onto something else. This is very powerful not only for creating quizzes, but also for non-scored interactions that are engaging and fun for the learner.

You can even take it further without programming or any complexity, but leveraging the built-in quiz variables to personalize the quizzing experience based on learner actions. And when it comes to reinforcing key concepts and messages, you have an unlimited variety of ways to provide this through feedback messages that are context-sensitive based on how the learner answers a question. Pretty cool stuff.

More information on quizzing techniques can be found in *Chapter 11, Rapid Development*. Next, we'll turn our attention toward some very interesting features that will help you add sizzle to your story!

9
Adding Visual Media to a Story

This chapter reviews the features of Storyline that enable external media assets to be incorporated into an e-learning course. The methods and supported file types are explored along with steps for importing media, working with web objects, and creating interactive software simulations with recorded video.

In this chapter, you will learn:

- How to work with media in Storyline
- Supported media
- How to import and embed media assets
- The basics of screen recordings, settings, and playback modes
- Creating emphasis with pans and zooms

Working with visual media

Media comes in many flavors; we've already touched on images in *Chapter 2, Adding Content into your Story* and in *Chapter 4, Adding Characters and Audio*, now we'll shift the focus to video. If a picture is worth a thousand words, then video is priceless. Video is one of the most effective tools to create an emotional impact. That is, if video is done well, produced properly, and for the right reasons (to support learning objectives).

Storyline handles a video well. There are a variety of options that allow you to bring video into your courses, and also perform basic editing tasks like trimming and cropping. Storyline also handles video compression very well, dramatically reducing the size of imported videos after publishing a course without degrading quality.

But that's not where things stop. You can use Storyline's video features to bring in elements that you have created in other tools, such as Articulate Studio, Quizmaker or Engage, as well as Adobe Flash and Captivate. You can even bring in content that you didn't create directly from the web, such as YouTube videos.

The net result is that you're able to not only re-use previously created content, but also expand your content by curating from the external sources. Powerful stuff indeed.

Supported media

Here are the video and audio formats that Storyline supports. Notice that video support includes **Flash video (FLV)** and **Flash interactions (SWF)**; these two formats are for desktop, rather than mobile playback.

Video	Audio
FLV, MP4, SWF	MP3
The following formats are converted to MP4 when they are imported:	All audio formats are converted to MP3 at 192 kbps when they are imported. Quality settings can be further adjusted before publishing
3G2, 3GP, ASF, AVI, DV, M1V, M2V, M4V, MOV, MPE, MPEG, MPG, QT, WMV	AAC, AIF, AIFF, M4A, OGG, WAV, WMA

Bringing media into a story – part 1

Storyline provides a few different methods for incorporating media into a story. Regardless of the method, you will begin from the **Insert tab** menu in the **Media** section of the Ribbon.

There are two ways to bring media into Storyline:

- **Insert into a slide**: With this method, content is imported into a slide. It can be edited, and its playback options can be adjusted.

- **Link to external content**: This method makes external content viewable within a slide or in a new browser window. When within a slide, it gives the appearance that content is contained directly within the slide, but in reality, it is only linked. The content cannot be edited but its playback can be adjusted.

How you choose to bring media into a story depends on what the media is and how it is intended to be used. Let's take a look at the first type of visual media, video.

Video

Video can be inserted from a file by navigating to a folder or network location where the video file is located and inserting it. Inserted video is treated like any other slide object. You can add Storyline playback controls to the video, and also place other slide objects on top of the video (great for annotating video). You can link to video from a website by using an embedded code to display it within a slide. This allows for seamless integration of external video content. If it's YouTube content, the video will be synchronized with the timeline, other web content will playback independent of the timeline.

Keep in mind that when linking to external content you will be subjected to the availability and format of the content.

You can record video from your computer's webcam and insert it into a slide. From the **Insert** menu, select the **Video** button and then choose **Record webcam...** You'll be prompted to select the camera device, recording size and audio device. You can record, stop, delete and preview the recording. Once inserted, you can then manipulate the recording as you would any video file that has been inserted into a slide by selecting it and choosing the **Options** menu.

Inserting video to a story

Follow these steps:

1. From the **Insert** tab, click on the **Video** button, choose **Video from file...** navigate to where the video is located, and choose **Open.**

2. The video appears on the slide. You can re-position and resize the video as you would any slide object. You can also adjust properties by selecting the video, choosing **Options** in the toolbar. The options include playback controls, alignment and sizing options.

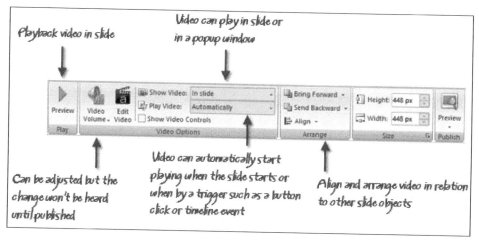

 When viewing a video in a slide, the learner can pause and play the video just by clicking on it. If you'd like to prevent this from happening, insert a transparent filled rectangle covering the video.

Editing video

Choosing **Edit Video** from the video **Options** menu produces the screen shown on the following page. Storyline provides basic editing capabilities. If you need advanced video editing, such as titling and transitions, it will be easier to do this with video editing software, such as Adobe After Effects or Premiere, and import the edited version of the video into Storyline.

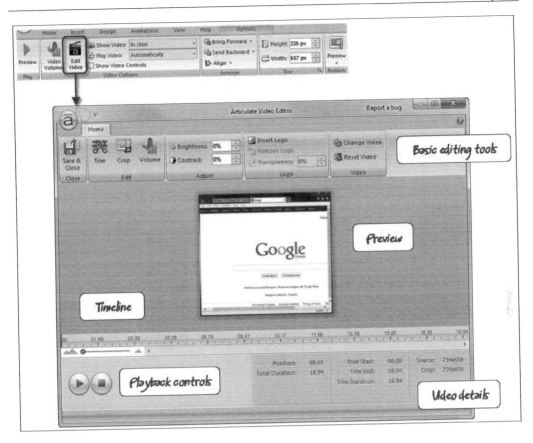

Basic tasks

Most of the time, video is supplied by the client and usually doesn't require editing. Sometimes though, you may need to touch up the video using the basic editing tools in Storyline's video editor. Here is a description of what you can do in Storyline:

- **Trim:** This controls the duration of the clip. You can trim the beginning and/or the end of the video by dragging the red trim markers in the video timeline. The duration is clipped to just the video in-between the beginning and end time markers.

- **Crop:** This is similar to cropping an image where you are adjusting the portion of the video that you would like to be visible to the learner. In the following example, the video of the car is cropped to just the car.

- **Insert Logo:** This lets you add an image that overlays the video with optional transparency.

- **Zoom:** This scales the video timeline up or down by dragging the slider that appears on the left side beneath the timeline.

- **Play, Stop, Volume, Reset** and **Save** are standard controls that allow you to work with live video as you perform basic editing tasks.

Inserting video from a website

Below are the steps to insert a video into your project from a website:

1. From the **Insert** tab, click on the **Video** button and select **Video from website...**.

2. Paste the embedded code from the external website and click on the **Insert** button.

The embed code is found in YouTube by clicking on the **Share** menu, and then **Embed**.

3. The video appears on the slide. You can re-position and resize the video. You can adjust properties by selecting the video choosing **Options** in the toolbar.

Any kind of media can be inserted into Master Slides. There may be times when you have a video clip that will be used on more than one slide, such as when a video plays in the background, as an ambient motion effect. For this kind of effect, you'll likely want to loop the video so that it doesn't end abruptly while the learner is viewing the slide. You can loop video and audio clips on a slide or master slide by using two triggers, one to play the media when the timeline starts, and the other to play the same media again, when the media completes. This will create an infinite loop until the slide timeline ends.

Follow along...

This exercise will expand upon the exercise completed in the previous chapter, where you will add a new scene into the project that will contain live video, flash, web site content and some interesting emphasis effects. Let's begin.

1. Open `Exercise 8 - Identity Theft` and choose **Save As...** and name it `Exercise 9 - Identity Theft`.

2. Let's add some new slides to work with, navigate to **Insert** and then **New Slide**. Choose the **Templates** tab, then from the **Template dropdown** menu, choose **Character Display Templates**.

3. Select **Flipchart**, **Project Screen**, **Folder** and **Laptop Screen**. From the **Insert into Scene** dropdown, choose **New Scene** and click on **Import**.

4. Switch to **Story View** and change the name of scene 1 to `Identity Theft` and scene 2 to `Security`.

5. Rename the newly inserted slides as follows:
   - Flipchart to `Security Measures`
   - Projection Screen to `Quiz`
   - Folder to `Browser`
   - Laptop Screen to `Warnings`

6. **Insert** a new slide after slide **2.4 Warnings** using the **Blank layout**. Name this `Introduction`.

7. **Insert** another new slide after **2.5 Introduction** using the **Title and Content layout**. Name this `Review`.

8. Switch to **Normal View** and navigate to **2.1 Security Measures**. Let's add some initial content to this slide by following the steps below:

    1. Change the **title** to `Browsing Securely on the Internet`.

    2. Add the following into the **content** placeholder.

       `This section of the course will focus on how you can prevent identity theft by browsing securely. To get started, take a moment to watch this video.`

    3. Insert a button, change the color to black/dark grey, add a play button icon and align it to the right then add the text `WATCH VIDEO` to the button.

9. The next step is to add a video into the project. With this video, we want to display it in a lightbox when the learner clicks the WATCH VIDEO button. We'll use slide 2.5 Introduction to contain the video then we'll come back and link the WATCH VIDEO button to this slide.

10. Navigate to slide **2.5 Introduction**.

11. Choose **Insert** from the menu, select the **Video** button and choose **Video from a website...**.

12. Outside of Storyline, open your web browser and go to `http://www.youtube.com/watch?v=KWTpz0UFmdA`. This is the video you will be inserting. To do this, you need to know what the embed code is. Click on **Share** and then, click **Embed**. Change the video size to 640 x 480 then copy all of the text inside the **Embed** text box.

13. Switch back to Storyline and press *Ctrl* + *V* to paste the embed code. Click on **Insert** to complete the process. The code should look like this:

    `<iframe width="640" height="480" src="http://www.youtube.com/embed/KWTpz0UFmdA?rel=0" frameborder="0" allowfullscreen></iframe>`

14. A video placeholder now appears in the slide. Re-size (enlarge) the video so that it fits the entire slide size by dragging the handles of the video placeholder.

15. In the timeline of the slide, move the video clip so that it starts at the .5 second mark and add a fade in animation to the video.

16. **Preview** this slide to see how the video plays back.

17. Navigate back to slide **2.1 Security Measures**. Add a trigger to the **WATCH VIDEO** button so that it lightboxes slide **2.5 Introduction** when the user clicks on the button.

18. **Preview** this scene and test the WATCH NOW button functionality.

19. **Save** the file.

 Be aware that if you insert YouTube video by using the **Insert video from a website** option, Storyline will wrap the video in a Flash control which means that the video will not play in HTML5 or on the Articulate Mobile Player application on an iPad. You might consider using a Web Object instead.

Bringing media into a story – part 2

Now let's take a look at two other types of media we can include in Storyline projects: Flash and external web content. We'll start with Flash.

Flash files

A Flash file (SWF) is typically brought into a Storyline project when an interaction is quite sophisticated and cannot be created in Storyline or the content already exists and is being re-purposed.

If the Flash file contains interactivity, such as a drag-and-drop exercise, you will need to insert the Flash file using the **Flash** button. However, if the Flash file doesn't contain any interactivity, then you can insert it using the **Video** button instead.

Adding Flash to a story

Follow these steps to add Flash into your project:

1. From the **Insert** tab, click on the **Flash** button for an interactive Flash file, or click on the **Video** button for a non-interactive file.

2. Navigate to where the Flash file is located and choose **Open**.

3. A placeholder appears on the slide (white, black or transparent). You can re-position and resize the Flash file as you would any slide object.

4. You can adjust the properties by selecting the placeholder choosing **Options** in the toolbar. The options include playback controls, alignment and sizing options.

Web content

This includes websites, blogs, wiki's, forums, RSS Feeds, Twitter, Facebook, Screenr – you name it, you got it. Almost everything on the web, including images and flash files can be viewed within a slide in Storyline. It doesn't have to be from the external web either, it can be html-based content in local folders or network drives.

You can include web content in two ways, by linking it within a slide or displaying it in a new browser window. The former will make it seem as if the content is directly on the slide. You can add scroll bars if the content is wider or longer than the slide size. You can have multiple web objects on a slide but keep in mind that web objects remain on top of other slide objects, even when placed on a master slide.

You can use the **Web Object** feature to incorporate interactions that you've created with other software, even legacy Flash content created with tools like Articulate Engage. These interactions, applications and websites will typically operate as expected since Storyline is just linking to the content, not interacting with it. The external content must work properly with iFrames in order for it to work properly within a web object. Note that Web Objects are supported in the Articulate mobile player for the iPad, as well as HTML5, however Flash content within, isn't.

Adding web content to a story

When inserting web content, Storyline looks for the start location, which will be a fully qualified URL like `http://www.articulate.com` or a local or network folder that contains web content. Web content folders include a starting file that Storyline will look for called `index.html`. If the starting file is named something different, like `index.htm` or `start.html`, you will need to rename it to `index.html`.

1. From the **Insert** tab, click on the **Web Objects** button and enter the web address where the content is located, or click on the **folder icon** to browse to a local file folder that contains web content.

2. Click on the **Test Link** button to ensure the content launches properly. By default, **Load Web Object automatically** is selected, you can uncheck this if you want the learner to be able to control when the content plays back.

 If the Web Object is set to not load automatically, you will likely want the placeholder to display a helpful image for learners. To do this, right-click the Web Object placeholder and select **Change Picture** then browse to the image you want to use, and click on **Open**.

3. Decide how to display the content, **in the slide** or in a **new browser window**. If a new browser window is chosen, you can display all browser controls, no address bar or no controls at all. You can also set the window size to anything you'd like.

4. Click **OK**. A placeholder appears that you can re-position and re-size.

Follow along...

Continuing with `Exercise 9 - Identity Theft`, let's insert variations of live web content into the Security section of our course.

1. Navigate to **2.2 Quiz** and change the title to `Security Quiz`.

2. Cisco, the hardware company, offers a variety of free security quizzes for the public. We're going to leverage this pre-made content into our course by carrying out the following the steps:

    1. Click on the **Web Object** icon in the content placeholder on the slide.

    2. Outside of Storyline, open your web browser and go to `http://newsroom.cisco.com/feature-content?type-webcontent&articleId=515300`. Beneath the video containing the quiz is the embed code. We don't need all of the code as we are concerned with just the SWF Flash file. Copy just the web address that follows **src=** in the embed code.

3. Switch back to Storyline and press *Ctrl + V* to paste the embed code. Click on the **Test Link** button to ensure the address is correct, and then click on **Insert** to complete the process. The address should look like this: `http://newsroom.cisco.com/documents/10157/2025611/SecurityQuiz4b.swf`.

4. Re-size the web object placeholder so that it appears to the right of the character that is on the slide.

5. **Preview** this slide to see how the web object behaves. Notice that Storyline doesn't allow a web object to be viewed when previewing. The story needs to be published, however, there is a workaround. Close out of Preview and right-click on the web object placeholder, and then choose **Preview**. You can preview this content *in the slide*. Clicking anywhere outside of the slide stops preview.

6. **Save** the file.

7. Now, let's move on to slide 2.3 Browser and add some information and instructions for an upcoming practice:

    1. Navigate to slide 2.3 Browser and change the title to `Ultra Safe Browsing`.

    2. Add a text box on top of the file folder with the following:

       `When you're finished reading the tips, click on the Next button to continue.`

8. Click the **Web Object** icon in the content placeholder and enter the web address of `http://www.dummies.com/how-to/content/top-ten-internet-security-tips.navId-323075.html?print=true` and click on **Insert**.

9. **Preview** the web object then **Save** the file.

Screen recordings and interactive simulations

Storyline includes a number of standalone tools included within the product, one of which is the **Screen Recording** tool. This tool has its roots in a complementary free service that Articulate offers, called Screenr (http://www.screenr.com).

Recording a screen

The screen recording tool allows you to record an area of your screen up to 2046 x 2046 pixels in size. Note that, if you have multiple monitors, you can only record on one monitor at a time. Recording happens from the **Insert** tab by clicking on the **Record Screen** button. A dashed outline of the area to record appears with controls along the bottom.

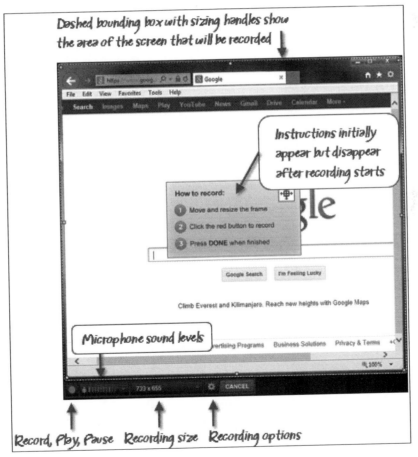

You'll see two dropdown menus along the bottom of the recoding screen with the following choices:

- **Recording size**: The default recording size is 720 x 540 pixels. This can be adjusted to 720 x 405 for a 16:9 ratio full screen, a select window, or a custom size, by adjusting the bounding box.

- **Microphone selection**: Storyline will use your default recording device, but you can change this by clicking on the down arrow that appears to the right of the sound volume indicator.

- **Recording options**: Clicking on the **gear** icon will display recording options. You can set up keyboard shortcuts to stop, pause/resume and take a screenshot by clicking in the boxes and pressing the desired key or key combination. You can also adjust microphone and speaker settings. Under Options, you can turn on the **Move new windows into recording area** so all windows that are opened while recording are captured. If the recording includes the system tray area of the screen, you can conceal the Storyline icon that appears there by checking **System tray icon**.

A recording can be used multiple times within a project and in more than one way:

- **As a video**: This inserts a non-interactive video for the learner to watch.

- **As a step-by-step demonstration**: Storyline understands when you have clicked the mouse and where, during a recording, these mouse click locations are converted to hotspots that can be used as an interaction where the learner must choose the right steps. The best example for a step-by-step recording would be a software simulation, but it's also useful for detailed diagrams and equipment simulations.

Steps to record a screen

Perform the following steps to record a screen:

1. Choose **Record Screen** from the **Insert** menu.

2. Adjust the bounding box to overlay the area you wish to record. You can also move the box by hovering over the lower left edge until a four-headed arrow appears, then click and drag the box without re-sizing it.

3. Click on the **Record** button to begin. A three second countdown appears before recording starts.

4. Record your steps then click on the **Done** button to finish the recording.

5. Give the recording a name.

6. Decide how to insert the recording, as a video or step-by-step slides.

7. Click on the **Insert** button.

Once a recording has been created, it is listed in the **Insert** menu under **Record Screen**. If it has already been inserted into the story, an **In Use** stamp will appear next to it.

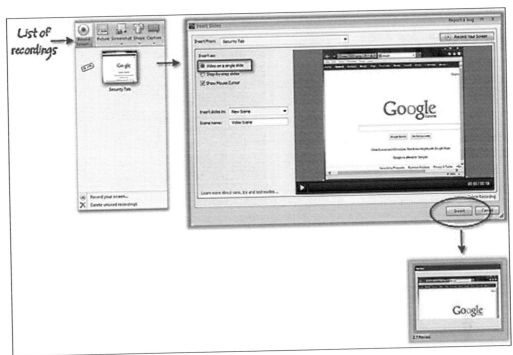

Step-by-step recordings inserted in View mode

View mode inserts a screen recording as a *demonstration* for learners and is not interactive. Learners can watch the process or production in action as Storyline annotates the original recording with captions and mouse click visuals and sounds.

As with all step-by-step recordings, the recording is edited and distributed over several slides, each slide containing a single interaction with feedback layers. It's best to create a new scene to house step-by-step recordings to which will help keep slide content organized.

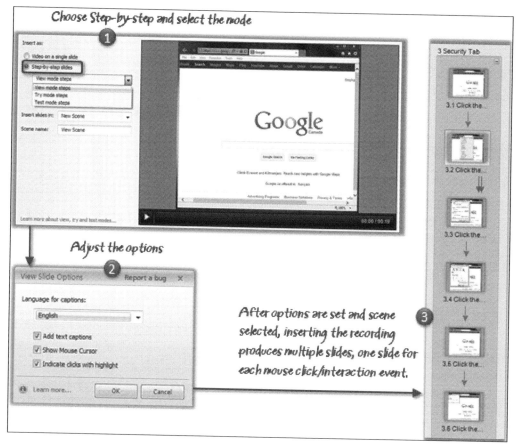

Step-by-step recordings inserted in Try mode

Try mode inserts a screen recording as an *ungraded assessment* allowing for the opportunity to practice steps. This type of recording is interactive and provides optional guidance, visual mouse cues, and correct feedback as the learner explores.

Step-by-step recordings inserted in Test mode

Test mode is a screen recording that is configured as a *graded exam*. This variation does not provide guidance or hints but offers both correct and incorrect feedback as the learner click on hotspots. A results slide can be optionally created upon completion and, as with other quiz types, you can limit the number of attempts the learner is able to try before correctly completing all steps.

Once a step-by-step recording has been inserted, you can edit the slides as you would any other slide – changing layout, adding objects, altering captions, hotspots and feedback.

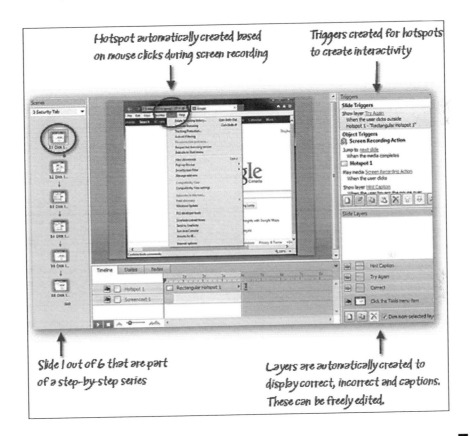

Hotspot automatically created based on mouse clicks during screen recording

Triggers created for hotspots to create interactivity

Slide 1 out of 6 that are part of a step-by-step series

Layers are automatically created to display correct, incorrect and captions. These can be freely edited.

If you are recording a web application or web page, it's recommended that you use Internet Explorer as it provides a rich set of data to the Windows Accessibility API. This is how Storyline collects information about your screen recording. Other browsers provide little information, so details will be missing from captions and steps might be omitted.

Fine tuning the recording

In some cases, you may need to fine tune the recording. Perhaps when it was recorded, there was a mistake made and you'd like to remove it, or perhaps the timing of a step is slightly off. In that case you can adjust the start and end frames of the recording through a feature called **Action Fine Tuning**. Here's how:

1. Navigate to the slide that you'd like to adjust in a step-by-step recording.

2. Right-click on the slide and choose **Action Fine Tuning**.

3. Just below the recording, in the playback area, drag the start frame and end frame markers along the timeline until the clip is showing just what you want to keep. You can also click on the `Previous Frame` or `Next Frame` buttons to move a frame at a time back or forward for precise selection.

4. Click on **Play** to preview how the slide will look. You can reset any changes made by clicking on the **Reset Original Timing** button, otherwise, select another slide from the dropdown menu if there's more editing to do, or click **OK** to finish.

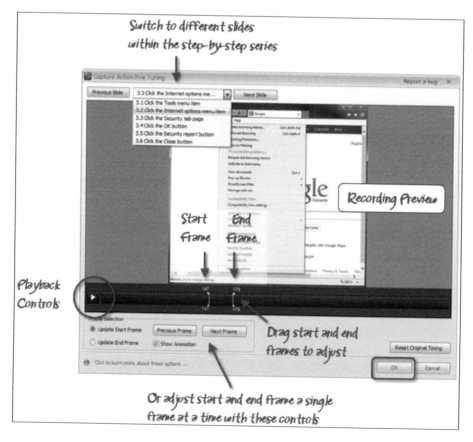

Follow along...

Continuing with `Exercise 9 - Identity Theft`, in this part of the exercise you will create an interactive software simulation that tests learner knowledge of key security features of a web browser.

1. Navigate to **2.4 Warnings** and change the title to **Browser Security**.

2. Add the following text on the laptop monitor:

   `It's your turn to practice. In this knowledge check you will need to locate the Security Options in the browser.`

3. Add a button with a play icon, aligned to the right, and with the words `BEGIN TEST`.

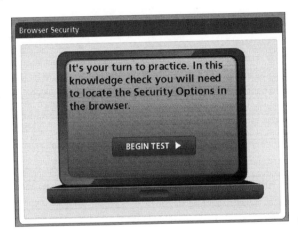

4. Outside of Storyline, open your web browser and re-size the window to be fairly small, about 800 x 600 – something close to what you think would fit width-wise in a Storyline slide. Go to `https://google.com` in the browser. We're going to record the steps to open the security tab in your browser. You might want to practice this. In Internet Explorer the steps would be **Tools | Internet Options | Security**. Switch back to Storyline when you're ready to record.

5. In Storyline, choose **Insert,** then **Record Screen** from the menu. Select **Record your screen...**.

6. Re-size and position the recording bounding box to cover the browser window.

7. Click on the **record** button and perform the steps to open the security tab.

   1. Move the mouse to the **Tools** menu and click.
   2. Select **Internet Options**.
   3. Select the **Security** tab.
   4. Click on **OK**.
   5. Move the mouse to the **LOCK** icon in the browser toolbar and click to view the details.
   6. Click the **X** to close the certificate details window.

8. Click on **Done** and name the recording, **Security Tab**.

9. Select **Step-by-step** and choose **Try Mode**.

10. Insert a new scene called **Security tab** and click on the **Insert** button.

11. Switch to **Story View**. Here you can see the new recording split over numerous slides in the new **Security Tab** scene.

12. Select this scene and **Preview** the scene. Test out the steps by making the correct choices then preview again making some mistakes so that you can see the feedback messages.

13. Double-click on the first slide in the step-by-step series and take a look at how the slide is set up. There should be a hotspot over the **Tools** menu in the screen recording that appears on the slide. Look in the **Triggers** panel and you'll find a trigger for that hotspot. Slide layers have automatically been created to **try again**, **correct**, and **hint** related messages. All the slide layers can be adjusted, in terms of look and feel, like you would a regular layer. You might want to look at how the other slides in the step-by-step series have been set up to familiarize yourself with what Storyline has done before continuing with the exercise.

14. Navigate to any slide in the step-by-step series then right-click on one of the recordings in a slide and choose **Action Fine Tuning...**, this opens an editor that lets you edit this portion of the overall recording. You can click on the **Play** button on the left side of the playback in this segment. Notice the timeline indicates the start and the end of just this portion of the step-by-step. You can drag those points forward or backward to fine tune exactly what should be viewed on this slide and for this portion of the interaction. We won't make any changes so you can click on the **Cancel** button to return to the slide.

15. Navigate to slide "2.4 Warnings" and add a trigger to the BEGIN TEST button so that it lightboxes slide "3.1 Click the Tools menu item" when the user clicks on it.

16. **Preview** the entire project. Try out the **BEGIN TEST** button to ensure it displays the step-by-step recording in a lightbox.

17. **Save** the file.

You can export a recording as an MP4 file or individual frames, by right-clicking in the preview area in the **Record Screen** menu.

Creating emphasis with pans and zooms

The Zoom feature within Storyline is a feature that you will find useful for creating emphasis without a lot of effort. This feature lets you give learners a close-up view of an area of the slide at any point during slide playback. You can time this with narration or sound effects and you
can create multiple zooms which, when set next to each other in the timeline, results in a panning effect.

You could use this feature to highlight content that is part of a detailed map or diagram, where zooming into a specific area lets the learner gain additional insight. It could also be used to give the learner a sense of heightened involvement, or to create dramatic emphasis during by zooming into an area that
the learner should be concentrating on.

Each zoom region can be sized and positioned wherever you'd like on the slide. All zoom regions appear in the timeline and each has a set start time and duration. If the zooms are not in order, use the timeline to move them around into the correct order. Unlike other objects in the timeline, multiple zoom regions remain on a single row and are executed from left to right. When a zoom ends, the screen reverts back to full size.

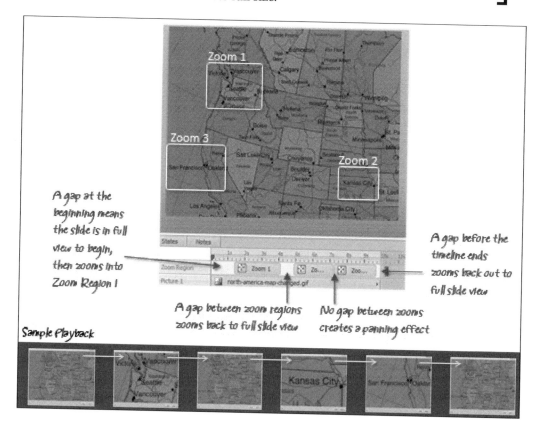

Follow along...

As a final touch to the `Exercise 9 - Identity Theft` course, you'll create a review slide that leverages the video that you've recorded to emphasize key browser settings.

1. Navigate to **2.4 Warnings** and change the player trigger in the **Triggers** panel from **jump to next slide** to **jump to slide 2.6 Review.**

2. Go to slide **2.6 Review** and view in **Normal view**.

3. Title the slide `Review`.

4. Choose **Insert** and then click on the **Record Screen** dropdown. Click on the screen recording that is listed then insert as **Video on a single slide**. Choose the **Security** scene to insert into, and then click on the **Insert** button.

5. Cut the video from the newly created **2.7 Untitled** slide by selecting it and pressing *Ctrl + X*, and then paste it into slide **2.6 Review** by pressing *Ctrl + V*. You can then delete slide **2.7 Untitled**.

6. Back on slide **2.6 Review**, resize the video so that it fits within the grey area of the slide, ensuring that it is aligned in the center of the slide.

7. Before we add the zoom effects, let's first edit the video to shorten it a bit. To do this, right-click on the video and choose **Edit Video**.

    1. Click on the **Trim** button.

    2. Drag the left trim marker in the timeline all the way back to the left side.

    3. Drag the right trim marker to about the 6 or 7 second mark. You'll need to play the video a few times to get the end point correct. We want the video to end before the Security tab window appears.

    4. Click on the **Crop** button and crop the video so just the upper half of the video will be visible on playback.

    5. Click on **Save & Close**.

8. Back on the slide, enlarge the video and align it so that it is centered on the slide.

9. Insert an oval shape to circle the https in the address bar. Change the color of the oval to red and add a shadow. Duplicate this and move the second copy over the top of the lock icon that is also in the address bar.

10. Next, let's add a zoom effect on this slide, so that when viewed, the slide will zoom up to the https, then pan over to the lock icon and then zoom back out to full size. To do this, follow these steps:

    1. Select **Insert,** then choose the **Zoom Region** button.

    2. A green bounding box appears on the slide, drag the handles and reposition this to cover the general area of where the **https** appears.

    3. Click on the **Zoom Region** button again and repeat for the **lock icon**.

11. In the **Timeline** panel, you will see two zoom region items along with the two ovals you inserted. We need to change the timing and duration of these elements. Use the image below as a guide.

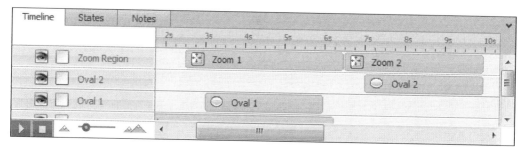

12. Preview the slide. If the zoom regions don't look right it could be that they are not in the right order. You can determine which zoom region is zooming first by selecting each on the timeline. Make sure that zooming to the https appears first (leftmost) in the timeline. To do this, locate the zoom object in the Timeline and drag it to the left so it appears before the other.

13. Let's also adjust the duration of the zoom transition to slow it down a little. Click on **Zoom 1** in the timeline, then on the slide, right-click anywhere in the zoom region box and choose **Zoom transition speed** and set it to **slow**. Repeat for the second zoom region.

14. **Preview** again to make sure it operates as you expect.

15. **Save** the file.

16. Change the player trigger in the **Triggers** panel on slide **1.6 Your Results** so that it jumps to slide **2.1 Security Measures** when the user clicks on the **Next** button.

17. Navigate to slide **2.1 Security Measures** and add a new trigger that jumps to slide **1.1 Instructions** when the user clicks on the **Previous** button.

18. **Preview** the entire project. Note that web objects will not be viewable during preview. Test the navigation of the course to make sure it functions properly and that the quizzes and other interactions are also functioning as expected. Make any tweaks you find necessary and **Save** the file.

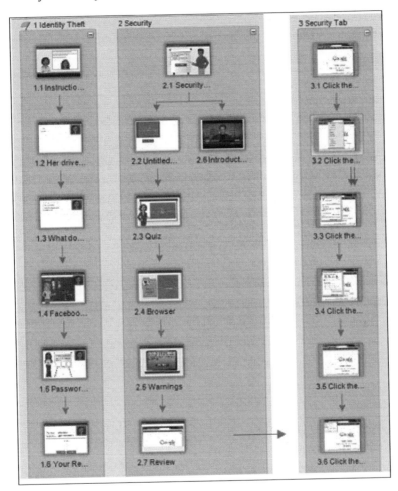

Tips on working with video

Here are some helpful pointers when working with video:

- Video doesn't necessarily mean actual video footage, it could be animations, motion infographics, self-running presentations and cartoon animations, such as those created with Code Baby or Xtranormal.

- If you know your way around PowerPoint, you can use its animation and transition effects to create sophisticated sequences, then export them as a movie. You can import the movies into Storyline as a `.wmv` file, or if you are using PowerPoint 2013, choose the `.mp4` format for reduced file size and seamless integration with Storyline.

- If you're working with actual video, and if the video is a talking head, where a person is talking without a lot of motion, then you may want to add a little creativity to encourage learners to pay attention. You can incorporate Storyline zoom regions, shapes, animations and other objects to the video as overlays or next to the video to annotate and visually reinforce what the person in the video is speaking about. The Storyline timeline lets you specify precisely when slide objects appear and disappear, so you can easily enhance a talking head video.

Summary

This chapter focused on ways that you can enhance your courses by incorporating a variety of visual media including video from the web and custom, interactive simulations. Video can be engaging, even a low-budget video can work well in an e-learning course, if it serves to enhance motivation or understanding of the subject matter.

Video done poorly comes off as an unnecessary bell and whistle. You'll want to make sure that other techniques, like animations, an information popup, or a link to a job aide, are considered first. If it can be done simpler without impairing the learning event, then it should be.

However, if video is the best choice then you need to decide, if you will create an original production from scratch or curate it from the vast volumes of publicly accessible media available on YouTube, Vimeo and other sources.

The techniques used in Storyline to incorporate video into your stories are also the same techniques you'd use to bring in other types of content from websites, blogs, forums, Twitter feeds and live web cams.

We've reached that special moment in a book when everything has come together. We've travelled from the very beginning to create a new course and arrived here, with a multimedia rich and interactive course. It's now time to publish so that we can share our courses with others!

10
Publishing your Story

This chapter takes a closer look at how a course looks when previewed and published. We'll take a look at the options that are available to customize colors and controls that surround course content and the methods and formats for publishing a course.

In this chapter, we will focus on:

- Previewing projects
- Customizing the player
- Publishing
- Publishing to the web
- Publishing with tracking
- Other publishing options
- Considerations

Previewing projects

While working through the various exercises contained in this book, you have had plenty of opportunity to use the preview feature. This is a helpful feature during the development process that allows you to view a sample of how a slide or scene is functioning without going through the publishing process. It's quick and dirty, particularly if you leverage the shortcut keys, *Ctrl + F12* to preview the current slide, *Shift + F12* for the current scene, and *F12* for the entire project.

Don't forget that preview doesn't mean save. Your project and all of your work will remain unsaved until you specifically choose the **Save** option. There is no autosave built into Storyline, so save often.

However helpful preview can be, there are some elements in your course that you won't be able to see while previewing. For those, you will need to publish in order to fully test functionality. Here's what can't be seen using preview:

- Web objects
- Videos inserted from websites
- Content imported from Articulate Engage
- Triggers containing JavaScript
- Hyperlinks
- Links to other slides that are not a part of the previewed range

Though you can't preview a web object using the preview feature, you can see it by right-clicking on the web object placeholder in the slide and choosing **Preview**. This shows the web object content but not the slide functionality, so it's a partial preview.

HTML 5 content can't be previewed in Storyline. When previewing, you'll always see the Flash version. To view the HTML 5 version, publish and launch it in a supported HTML 5 browser. You can also manually locate the `story_html5.html` file in the root of the published output to launch the HTML 5 version. The same applies for the IOS or iPad version.

Customizing the Player

When you previewed the exercises in this book, you probably noticed that course content, words, media, and other objects on a slide, were surrounded by an interface. This is called the **Player** and it can be as minimal as a 10 pixel border all the way around a course or more elaborate to include logos, menus, and playback controls.

You can make the player transparent by giving the illusion that there is no player at all by adjusting the player colors; `Base bg`, `Base border`, and `Base slide_bg` are set to 100 percent transparent.

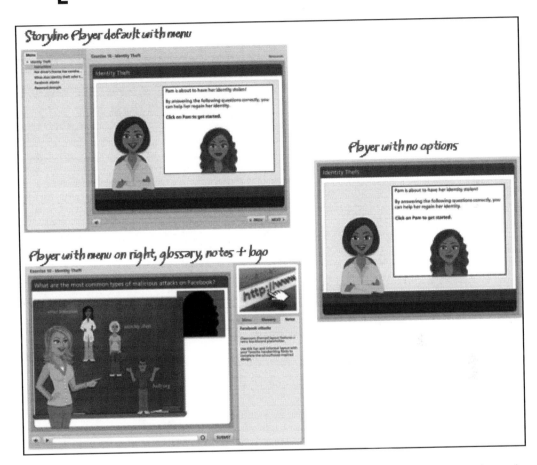

What's really great with this feature is that Storyline lets you fully customize how the Player looks and what features appear on it. You can then save that setup and reuse the player with other Storyline projects; a big time saver and a great way to deliver consistent results.

Customizing the player is done by clicking on the **Player** option from the **Home** tab. Player options are wide and varied; we'll highlight some of the features you should be aware of and take some time to get to understand better. First, let's take a look at the player interface:

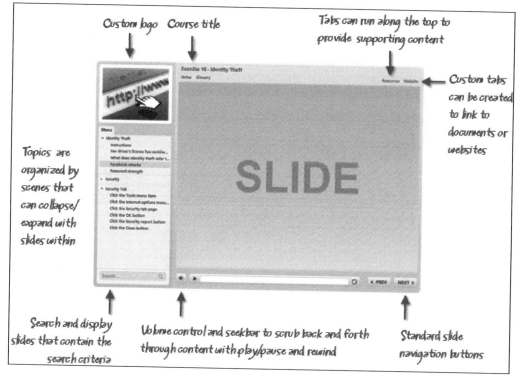

Player properties review

After clicking on the **Player** option, a number of properties appear and they are organized in three sections in the RIbbon at the top; layout, data, and custom.

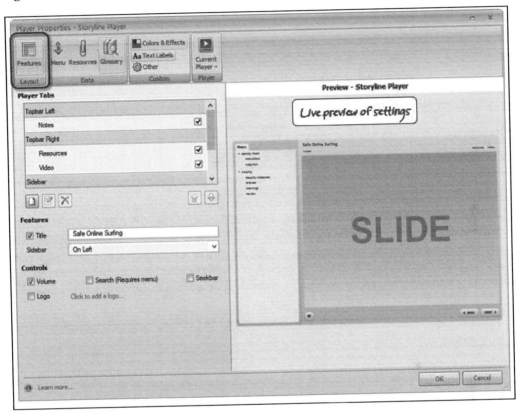

Features

You can rename, remove, add, and reposition the **Player** tabs that appear along the top and sides of the player from this area. This is a powerful feature that can be used to make various forms of supporting content available to learners at any point during the course. The **Controls** area at the bottom of the **Properties** window defines the default appearance for playback controls for all slides in the story. Most of the options here can be overridden at the slide-level with the exception of volume, search, and logo. Make sure that the **Course Title**, if checked, isn't left blank or contains special characters or symbols, as this is known to cause issues with some LMS's.

Menu

When the **Menu** tab is enabled in the **Features** area, a menu option appears showing the learner what's inside the course. By default, each scene and the slides within are grouped using the names of the scenes and slides as depicted in the story itself.

You would usually make adjustments for how the menu content appears by using friendly scene and slide names, and removing slides the learner doesn't need to see listed in the menu or have direct access to. An example might be to remove subtopic slides leaving just the major topics visible from the course menu. Removing a slide from the menu doesn't delete the content, it just hides it from displaying as an item in the menu.

In the following example, the left column shows that the course menu, by default, lists all of the scenes and slides in the course. After some adjustments, the middle column shows only two of the three scenes and fewer slides. The right-most column shows how these menu adjustments look when published:

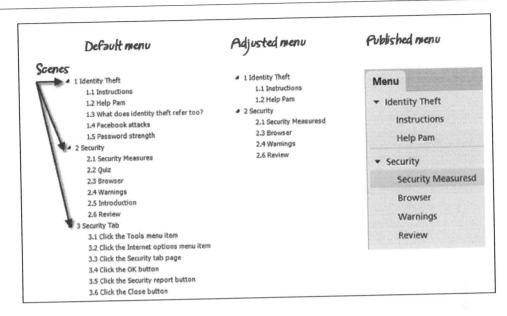

You can change the name of the scenes and slides and re-order them. Renaming slides in the menu does not change the actual slide names used in the story. In fact, any adjustments you make to how the menu is displayed will not affect the functionality of the course or the presentation order of the content.

The menu shows slide numbering alongside the slide name. If you re-order slides, the numbering can appear to be out of sequence. This number sequencing doesn't actually appear to the learner, by default, no menu appears at all. You can adjust this in **Menu Options** by clicking on the gear icon in the lower right corner and checking the number entries in the menu automatically. When you do this, numbering appears sequential to the learner.

Also within **Menu Options**, the **Navigation Restriction** drop-down controls how the learner moves through a course. The default is Free, meaning learners can use the back and next buttons as well as the menu to view the presentation in any order they'd like. You can change this to Restricted so learners are able to move backward but can't skip ahead or you can choose Locked which forces learners to view content in the order you've designed. They won't be able to move backward or forward unless there is a specific trigger allowing them to do so.

The Following is a screenshot of the **Menu** options that are accessed by clicking on the **Gear** icon:

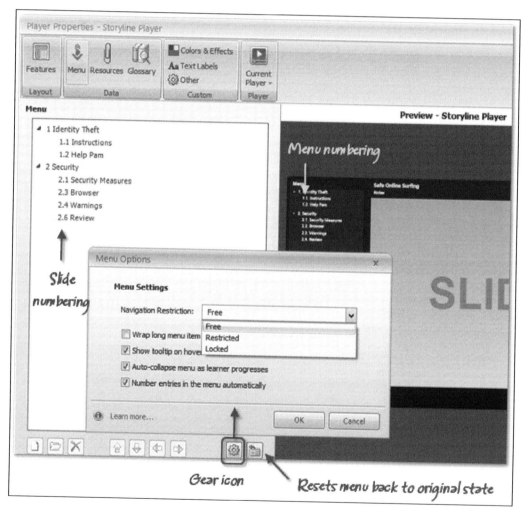

Resources

This feature lets you attach supporting content, such as file attachments and links in the **Resources** tab that appears at the top of the **Player**. Content contained in any **Player** tab is accessible throughout the course.

Glossary

The glossary lets you include terms and definitions. This content, though accessible throughout the course, is not directly linked to any terms that may appear within the slide content.

Colors and effects

You can alter the color of the player by switching from one built-in theme to another. You can also alter a theme and create new themes with individual color changes for various elements similar to how you would alter other theme colors found in Storyline and PowerPoint. What's interesting is that you can control the transparency levels for almost all elements, allowing for greater design options. You can save a color scheme so that it can be used for other Storyline projects.

Text labels

This feature lets you customize the default text that appears in the player and the course. For example, you may want the **Notes** tab to appear as transcript or the **Previous** button to be called **Back** instead. Storyline supports multiple languages as well.

Other

This option lets you specify how a published course appears in a browser. The options you set here will relate to the size and design of your story as well as the quality of media within. You can allow the learner to maximize the browser window and have the course scale to fill the window. Storyline stretches the content to achieve this effect. Since Storyline content is raster not vector, lower resolution images may appear fuzzy when stretched beyond their original dimensions. You can lock the player at an optimal size so that the course won't stretch, but if your story size is 720 x 540 and it's being played back on a large, high resolution monitor it will appear quite small.

You can set the **Resume** option so that when a learner returns to the course, Storyline will prompt to resume, so they can choose to pick up from where they left off, or this can be set so the course always automatically resumes, or never resumes. This can be further configured so the resume action occurs only if the course is running in an LMS.

Current Player

This option lets you save the current player settings, along with the glossary and resources, as a new player that can be used for other Storyline projects that you work on. You can also share players with other Storyline users by leveraging the import and export options found here.

Follow along...

In this exercise you will work with the player to configure some of the settings. Following the exercise, there is a list of the key player properties that you can review.

1. As a first step, open `Exercise 9 - Identity Theft` and save it as `Exercise 10 - Identity Theft`.

2. Click the **Player** button on the **Home** tab. You can see in the preview windows that all of the scenes in this project along with all of the slides are visible in the menu. We don't want the learner to see everything, so let's work with the menu to tidy this up:

    1. Click on the **Menu** tab

    2. Rename the 1.2 menu item to be `Help Pam`

    3. Delete menu items 1.3, 1.4, and 1.5 by selecting each and clicking on the red **x** delete button at the bottom of the window. Remember deleting here doesn't delete the actual slide, just the items in the menu list in the player.

    4. Delete **2.2 Quiz** and **2.5 Introduction**; we don't want learners to jump to the quiz, and the introduction is a video that appears in a lightbox so it shouldn't be visible in the menu.

    5. Delete the entire last scene with children (slides), scene 3 **Security Tab**, as this is the step-by-step interaction that the learner will get from a link on another slide so it doesn't need to appear in the menu. Notice that the preview window is updating as you are making changes.

3. Select the **Features** tab and navigate to **Notes** to include any details that appear in the **Notes** panel on each slide. Note that content is edited on each slide in the **Notes** area and typically is used as a transcript for voice narration but can include any text.

4. Navigate to the **Notes** item, then using the up arrow (beneath the **Player** tab) click it several times so the **Notes** tab appears in the top bar left section. Look at the preview window to see if it is correctly positioned. You can also click on the tab to see how it looks expanded.

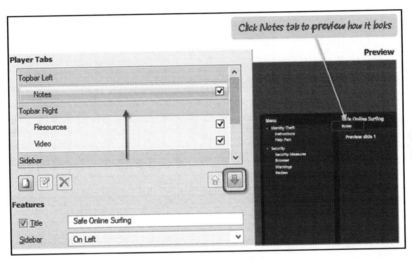

5. Add a resource by clicking on the **Resource** tab and then click on the **New Item** icon in the lower left corner. Enter the Articulate website address of `www.articulate.com` and click on **Test** to make sure it works and then click on **Save**.

6. It would be great to provide the introduction video to learners no matter where they are in the course as a quick reminder of some of the key messages. Let's add a new custom tab to the player to achieve this:

    1. Click on the **Features** tab and then click on the **New Item** icon that appears beneath the **Player** tab.

    2. Type the tab name as `Video` then set it so that Storyline places the **2.5 Introduction** slide into a lightbox when the user clicks on the tab.

7. Click on **Colors and Effects** and change the **Color Scheme** to **Black**.

8. Click on **OK** to save the player changes.

9. Preview the entire project and note the player changes, particularly the custom **Video** tab, link in the resources tab (which won't work during preview), and the **Notes** tab.

10. While still previewing, navigate to the **Review** slide in the **Security** section. Notice that the recorded video plays back but there aren't any controls on the player to allow the learner to pause this video. This is where preview can really help you fix things as you go. We caught this problem, so let's change it:

　　1. Close out of preview and switch to **Story View**

　　2. Navigate to the **2.6 Review** slide and on the right side under **Player Features**, select **Custom** for the selected slide

　　3. Check the **Seekbar** option.

　　4. **Preview** just this slide to ensure the seekbar is visible and you can control the recorded video.

　　5. **Save** the file.

Publishing

When the time comes to fully test your course in the environment it will reside in, you will need to publish the project. This is typically done locally using one of the five available publishing formats: Web, Articulate online, LMS (Learning Management System), CD, or Word. Once published, the resulting files and folders are usually copied to a web folder, network location, or LMS.

The first time a project is published, it will take a few minutes to complete in order to generate the necessary files and folders as well as optimize and compress audio and video files. Subsequent publishing will go a little faster.

Published output

Storyline doesn't publish a single file, it actually creates hundreds of files contained in a few folders. The entire published output folder structure will need to be copied to the hosting destination in order for the course to operate correctly.

Here is an example of the published output folder:

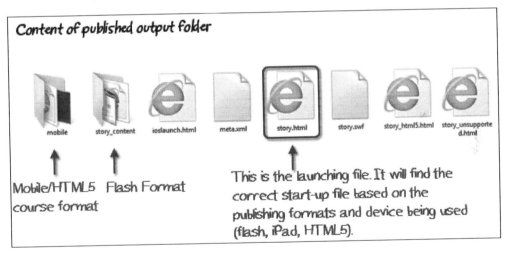

Publishing to the web

Use the **Publishing to the Web** option when you'd like the course to be accessible on the web or an internal intranet and you don't need to track learner progress or completion.

1. To begin, from the **Publish** tab, navigate to the **Web** option and give the course a **Title** and a **Description**.

2. Enter the optional details by clicking on the ellipses buttons to the right of **Title**.

3. Choose a publish location. By default this is **Documents\My Articulate Projects** but you can change this by clicking on the ellipses next to the **Folder** location box.

4. Decide if you are going to include support for HTML 5 devices and/or the **Articulate Mobile Player** app for the iPad.

5. Adjust the player to be used, if needed, and the quality settings to fine tune audio and video compression.

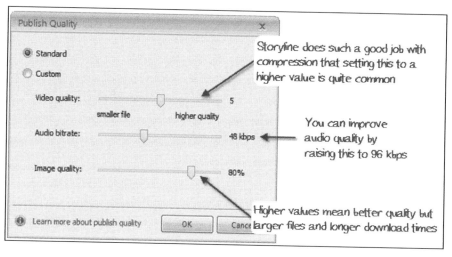

6. Click on **Publish**.

7. After publishing is complete, a window appears notifying you that the publishing process was successful. You can then view the published course or you can e-mail, ftp, zip it, or open the folder where the published output files are located.

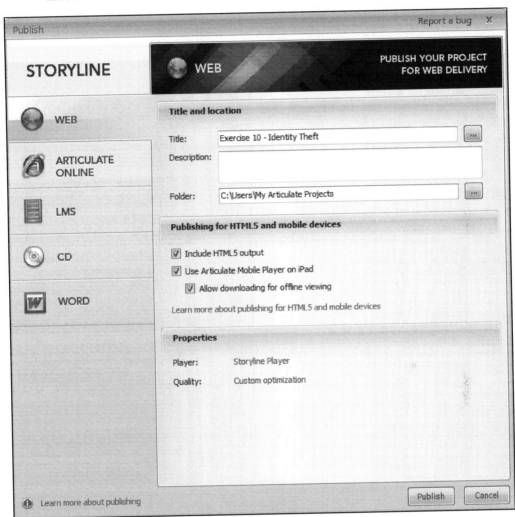

Publishing to the Web, Articulate Online, LMS, or CD offers the ability to include HTML 5 and iPad support. If you choose both, here's how Storyline determines which version of the course to display:

- If the learner is using a Flash compatible browser, the Flash version will be displayed

- If the learner is using an iPad, the course will be displayed in the Articulate Mobile Player app

- If the learner is using a non-Flash compatible browser, the HTML 5 version will be displayed

You may find that viewing a published Storyline project on your local computer does not work as expected. This may be due to local security restrictions on your computer, the Flash player, or browser security. To view a published story locally on a Windows PC without security restrictions, you can use the **Publish for CD** option instead and launch the course using the Launch_Story.exe file.

Follow along...

The time has come to publish our story. In this exercise you will publish to the web without tracking. Some additional information and considerations that you should be aware of will follow this exercise.

1. Let's start by opening Exercise 10 - Identity Theft and clicking on the **Publish** button from the **Home** tab.

2. Adjust the **Title** to be **Safe Online Surfing**.

3. Click on the **ellipsis** next to the title and enter any other details you wish to further describe the course. This is particularly useful for courses that are hosted on a tracking system.

4. Add the **Description** of a primer on operating securely on the Internet.

5. Select the folder to contain the published output.

It's wise to avoid publishing on a network. Instead, publish locally to prevent publishing errors, then copy or upload the published output to a shared network location, web server, or LMS.

6. Click on **Publish**.

7. When the completion prompt appears, click on **View Project** to review the course and test functionality.

8. When you return to Storyline, close the completion prompt, and save the file.

9. Outside of Storyline, navigate to the folder where the published output is located. The published output will be in a folder called `Safe Online Surfing` output. Take a look at the files and note that you can launch the course again by double-clicking on the `story.html` file.

Publishing with tracking

You'll need an LMS to capture tracking and completion information. Storyline can publish to **Articulate Online**, its own LMS, or an LMS of your choice. The options between the two are similar with the exception of tracking; when publishing to an LMS you can choose from several output formats, including SCORM 1, 2, SCORM 2004, AICC, or Tin Can API. In all cases, you'll need to identify how reporting and tracking will be handled:

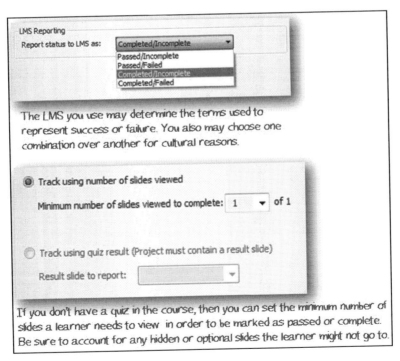

Considerations when tracking

You will want to keep in mind the following points when working with your course and adjusting tracking settings:

- If you do not have a quiz in your course and must mark the course as complete, you can do this as mentioned earlier by setting the number of slides viewed. If you need more precision, you can create a hidden quiz question and use the associated results slide for course completion. Here is a tutorial on how to do this http://www.articulate.com/support/kb_article.php?product=st1&id=8bi7nnp5g3z7.

- If you have a single quiz, you can record learner completion based on the associated results slide.

- If you have multiple quizzes, you can use only one results slide to mark the course as passed or completed.

- If you are using the Tin Can API, the quiz result slide you select will report overall results that includes individual questions from all quizzes and results slides.

Other publishing options

Storyline includes two other publishing options. The first option is **Publish to CD**, which creates a version of the course that launches from an executable file. This can be used for CD, DVD, or USB drive playback.

The other option is **Publish to Word**. This is actually quite handy for review cycles during development. A document is created that contains each slide, and optionally slide layers along with slide notes. This includes quizzes with possible options and the correct choices. It creates a visual transcript of a course and is a terrific feature you can leverage to speed up documentation effort and content review processes for your course.

Considerations when working with HTML 5 output

The biggest challenge when it comes to publishing is playback on HTML 5 browsers and mobile devices. The iPad generally works quite well when launching courses from the **Articulate Mobile Player** app (downloaded for free from the App Store).

Playback outside of Flash-based browsers or the iPad app, is fairly limited. This is due, in part, to the infancy of the HTML 5 standard. HTML 5 is not fully implemented and each browser and platform/device handles things slightly differently, making it challenging to create one course and have it operate as expected across multiple browsers, platforms, and mobile devices. You'll get close by simplifying your course content and removing content features that aren't supported across all platforms, or by creating multiple versions optimized for the target environments.

The Appendix provides a link to a detailed chart of feature support when working with Flash, HTML 5 and iOS (iPad output).

Summary

Storyline makes it easy to publish a course and customize the way it appears when published. It does this with simplicity and offers enough options to help you tailor the experience so that it fits your design and cultural requirements.

Being able to save a player and re-use this for other Storyline courses is a great time saver. Sharing with other developers helps create consistency within development teams.

The many configuration settings offer another way to create original, custom experiences for your learners. You might consider creating several players to suit different types of courses as follows:

- Sidebar menu visible with restricted navigation for linear courses
- No **Previous** and **Next** buttons for courses with custom navigation built within the Slide Masters.
- No seekbar for courses that contain video clips with their own controls to play, pause, step, and replay the video.
- Chromeless, which means every player option is disabled leaving only a 10 pixel border around the slide content that can also be made transparent leaving just the slide without any player controls at all. This is a crisp and clean format that's great for self-running presentations or courses with your own custom navigation built within the slide content.

The next chapter offers some advice to help you make the most from what you've learned about Storyline.

11
Rapid Development

Rapid development is about how you can easily reuse, share, and edit e-learning assets to expedite development of courses. This chapter provides some thoughts on using Storyline effectively to produce quality results while increasing your productivity.

In this chapter you will learn:

- The concept of reusability in Storyline
- Methods of leveraging existing assets
- How to build once, and reuse many times
- Best practices for organizing assets
- Key productivity boosters in Storyline

Concept of reusability

The concept of reusability has its roots in the production process. Typically, most of us go about creating e-learning using a process similar to what is shown in the following screenshot. It works well for large teams and the one man band, except in the latter case, you become a specialist for all the stages of production. That's a heavy load. It's hard to be good at all things and it demands that you constantly stretch and improve your skills, and find ways to increase the efficiency of what you do.

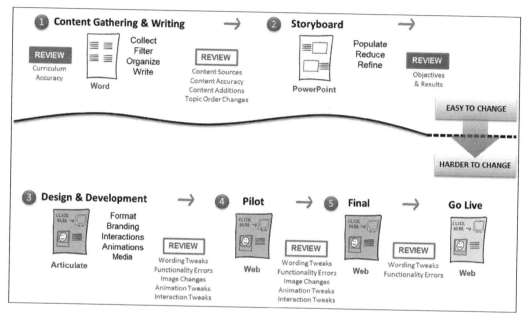

Reusability in Storyline is about leveraging the formatting, look and feel and interactions you create so that you can re-purpose your work and speed-up production. Not every project will be an original one-off, in fact most won't, so the concept is to approach development with a plan to repurpose 80 percent of the media, quizzes, interactions, and designs you create. As you do this, you begin to establish processes, templates, and libraries that can be used to rapidly assemble base courses. With a little tweaking and some minor customization, you'll have a new, original course in no time. Your client doesn't need to know that 80 percent was made from reusable elements with just 20 percent created as original, unique components, but you'll know the difference in terms of time and effort.

Leveraging existing assets

So how can you leverage existing assets with Storyline? The first things you'll want to look at are the courses you've built with other authoring programs, such as PowerPoint, QuizMaker Engage, Captivate, Flash, and Camtasia.

If there are design themes, elements, or interactions within these courses that you might want to use for future Storyline courses, you should focus your efforts on importing what you can, and further adjusting within Storyline to create a new version of the asset that can be reused for future Storyline courses. If re-working the asset is too complex or if you don't expect to reuse it in multiple courses, then using Storyline's web object feature to embed the interaction without re-working it in any way may be the better approach. In both cases, you'll save time by reusing content you've already put a lot of time in developing.

Importing external content

Here are the steps to bring external content into Storyline:

1. From the **Articulate Startup** screen or by choosing the **Insert** tab, and then **New Slide** within a project, select the **Import** option.
2. There are options to import PowerPoint, Quizmaker, and Storyline. All of these will display the slides within the file to be imported. You can pick and choose which slides to import into a new or the current scene in Storyline.
3. The **Engage** option displays the entire interaction that can be imported into a single slide in the current or a new scene.
4. Click on **Import** to complete the process.

Considerations when importing

Keep the following points in mind when importing:

- PowerPoint and Quizmaker files can be imported directly into Storyline. Once imported, you can edit the content like you would any other Storyline slide. Master slides come along with the import making it simple to reuse previous designs. Note that 64-bit PowerPoint is not supported and you must have an installed, activated version of Quizmaker for the import to work.

The PowerPoint to Storyline conversion is not one-to-one. You can expect some alignment issues with slide objects due to the fact that PowerPoint uses points and Storyline uses pixels. There are 2.66 pixels for each point which is why you'll need to tweak the imported slides just a bit. Same with Quizmaker though the reason why is slightly different; Quizmaker is 686 x 424 in size, whereas Storyline is 720 x 540 by default.

- Engage files can be imported into Storyline and they are completely functional, but cannot be edited within Storyline. Though the option to import Engage appears on the **Import** screen, what Storyline is really doing is creating a web object to contain the Engage interaction. Once imported into a new scene, clicking on the Engage interaction will display an **Options** menu where you can make minor adjustments to the behavior of the interaction as well as **Preview** and **Edit** in it Engage. You can also resize and position the interaction just as you would any web object. Remember that though web objects work in iPad and HTML5 outputs, Engage content is Flash, so it will not playback on an iPad or in an HTML5 browser. Like Quizmaker, you'll need an installed, activated version of Engage for the import to work.

- Flash, Captivate, and Camtasia files cannot be imported in Storyline and cannot be edited within Storyline. You can however, use web objects to embed these projects into Storyline or the **Insert Flash** option. In both cases, the imported elements appear seamless to the learner while retaining full functionality.

Storyline Project Leveraging Existing Assets

Slide 1 – Created in Storyline (drag & drop), remaining slide content was imported from various sources resulting in a media, fully interactive course.

Slide 2 – Captivate Scenario

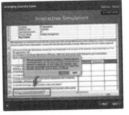

Slide 3 – Camtasia Simulation

Slide 4 – Flash Interaction

Slide 5 – Web Content

Slide 6 – PPT Animation

Slide 7 – Imported Video

Build once, and reuse many times

Quizzing is at the heart of many e-learning courses where often the quiz questions need to be randomized or even reused in different sections of a single course (that is, the same questions for a pre and post-test). The concept of building once and reusing many times works well with several aspects of Storyline. We'll start with quizzing and a feature called **Question Banks** as follows:

Question Banks

Question Bank offers a way to pool, reuse, and randomize questions within a project. Slides in a question bank are housed within the project file but are not visible until placed into the story. Question Banks can include groups of quiz slides and regular slides (that is, you might include a regular slide if you need to provide instructions for the quiz or would like to include a post-quiz summary).

When you want to include questions from a Question Bank, you just need to insert a new **Quizzing** slide, and then choose **Draw from Bank**. You can then select one or more questions to include and randomize them if desired.

Follow along...

This exercise will use the sample project file created in *Chapter 8* called, Exercise 8 - Identity Theft. This should be open in order to begin the exercise. You will be removing three questions from a scene and moving them into a question bank. This will allow you to draw one or more of those questions at any point in the project where the quiz questions are needed, as follows:

1. From the **Home** tab, choose **Question Banks**, and then **Create Question bank**. Title this **Identity Theft Questions**.

2. Notice that a new tab has opened in **Normal View**. The Question Bank appears in this tab. Click on the **Import** link and navigate to question slides 2, 3, and 4. From the **Import** drop-down menu at the top, select **move questions into question bank**.

3. Click on the **Story View** tab and notice the three slides containing the quiz questions are no longer in the story. Click back on the **Identity Theft** tab and notice that they are located here. The questions will not become a part of the story until the next step, when you draw them from the bank.

4. In Story View, click once on slide 1 to select it, and then from the **Home** tab, choose **Question Banks** and **New Draw** from **Question Bank**.

5. From the **Question Bank** drop-down menu, select **Identity Theft Questions**. All questions will be selected by default and will be randomized after being placed into the story. This means that the learner will need to answer three questions before continuing onto the next slide in the story. Click on **Insert**.

6. The Question Bank draw has been inserted as slide 2. To see how this works, **Preview** the scene.

7. **Save as** Exercise 11 - Identity Theft Quiz.

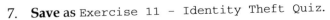

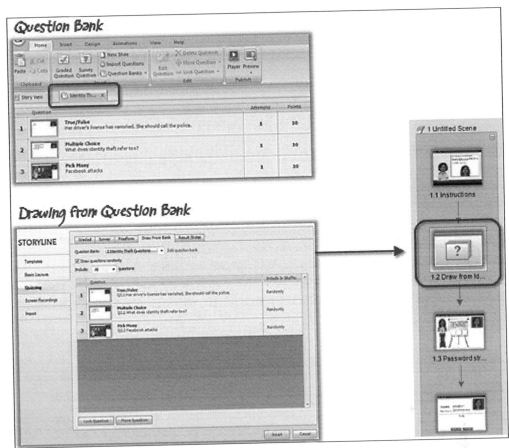

There are multiple ways to get back to the questions that are in a question bank. You can do this by selecting the tab the questions are located in (in this case, **Identity Theft**), you can view the question bank slide in Normal View or choose **Question Banks** from the **Home** tab and navigate to the name of the question bank you'd like to edit.

Interaction templates

Whether a question or interaction is created from scratch, from templates that came with Storyline, or that someone else provided you will likely modify it to suit your needs. To reuse a question or interaction, you can save it in a Storyline file by itself and then import it into a project. All formatting, media, animations, and triggers will come along with it.

 Keep in mind that the slide size matters, for example, if you save the template as 720x540 and import this into a project with dimensions of 720x405, images will be stretched to adapt to the 16:9 ratio.

Follow along...

You created an interaction in *Chapter 6, Using Variables to Customize the Learning Experience* that asked the learner to type their thoughts, and then displayed those thoughts alongside the feedback. This is a common interaction that could be used in many projects. Let's save it out on its own then bring it into our Identity Theft Quiz. We'll start this exercise with a new, blank project as follows:

1. With a new, blank project opened, select **New Slide** from the **Home** tab, choose **Import** and navigate to **Storyline**. Locate Exercise 6 - Sales Training and click on **Open**.

2. Select **None** in the upper-right corner of the Import window to deselect all slides, and then navigate to the **Module 1** section and select just the **Details** slide.

3. Select **import into Current Scene**, and then click on the **Import** button.

4. Delete the first blank slide.

5. On the newly imported slide, in the **Triggers** panel, delete the **Slide Trigger** (set Mod1Complete...) and **Player Trigger** (jump to...).

6. **Save** this as Exercise 11 - User Thought Interaction.

7. Open Exercise 11 - Identity Theft Quiz and select the last slide.

8. Let's bring in the interaction by selecting the **Insert** tab and choosing **New Slide** then **Import**. Select **Storyline** and locate Exercise 11 - User Thought Interaction. Only one slide will be selected, choose to import this into the **Current Scene** and click the **Import** button.

9. Open the **TextEntry** trigger that displays in the **Trigger** panel on the newly imported interaction and change the variable to Thoughts.

10. **Preview** the slide and test functionality.

11. **Save** the file.

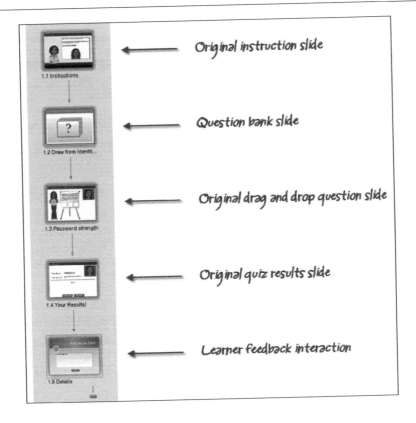

Reusing glossaries and resources

The Storyline Player includes tabs that contain glossary terms and definitions as well as resources for links to supporting documents and websites. What if you want to use the same glossary to resources listing in more than one project?

You might think that, by saving the **Player**, the glossary and resources will also be saved with it, however, this isn't what happens. The glossary and resources stay with the project and not the Player.

To reuse these items you will need to save the current project as a template by selecting the **Articulate file** icon (upper-left corner of the Storyline window) and choosing **Save As...**, and then select the **Storyline template** from the file type drop-down menu. When the template is used to create a new project, the glossary and resources will come along with it (note that this works only when creating new projects with the template).

Reusing characters and images

The **Characters** feature in Storyline is terrific for being able to insert high quality cutout images of people into your e-learning courses. The fact that there are so many poses and expressions lends itself to all sorts of creative ways to use these images.

The characters are available in every project, but how they are set up in terms of poses and expressions needs to be manually configured each time you use a character. For example, if you use a female character that is in a happy pose, but when clicked changes to a confused pose, that means you have two states for the character. If you want to use this character with these states in another project, you'll need to manually re-create it, unless you save the characters in a file and import them into a project.

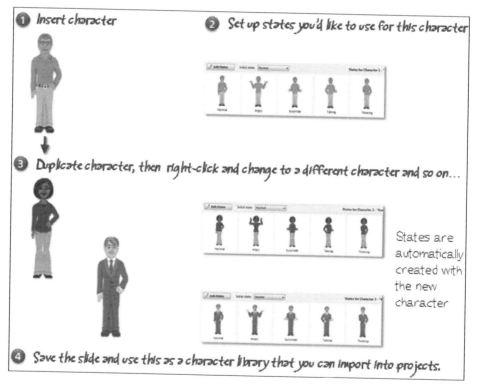

Creating images from video

Another useful way to reuse existing media is to create images from video clips that you may have for a project. Instead of spending time trying to locate fresh images, why not create them from video footage you already have You can do this using the technique shown here:?

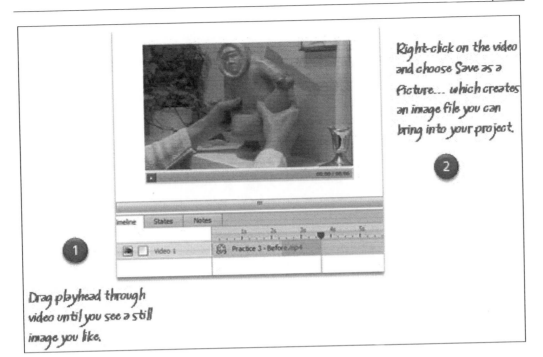

Best practices for organizing assets

It doesn't take long to accumulate a large volume of files for a given project. You can save a lot of time and frustration by keeping the following points in mind as you set out to develop and manage e-learning courses:

- Establish and adhere to a file naming convention and use this consistently.

- Establish a versioning system and use this frequently and consistently, bring the version number right into the beginning slide so there is no confusion about which version is being worked on.

- Create a master folder structure and copy this when starting a new project. This ensures that the image files are placed in an image folder, documents and scripts in another folder, and so on. Use this structure locally and on a network if you are working with others.

- Use a style kit to define the branding, colors, fonts, and template elements. This is the single source for definitive information regarding the use of your client's images, logos, and brand in the context of the design you have created for the Storyline project. Version this style kit like you would the master Storyline project files.

- Create a companion PowerPoint elements file that contains all the original graphics and animations you may have created in PowerPoint then brought into Storyline. Doing this will help you save time editing down the road when changes are needed for these elements.

- Establish a master or global folder structure that all projects can draw from. This might contain folders for commonly used fonts, logos, sounds, images, production process templates, Photoshop files, and so on.

- Place into that master or global folder a living document called *Storyline Best Practices and Tips*. This could be done using OneNote or EverNote, so you can easily capture images, bookmarks, and other elements as you discover new tips. You'll be amazed how many timesavers and workarounds there are, not to mention interesting new ways of developing in Storyline. You'll want to keep a list of these items; perhaps organized by production process, development, graphics, audio, video, animation, and so on. Increase the value of this curated information by having the whole production time contribute to the shared knowledge base.

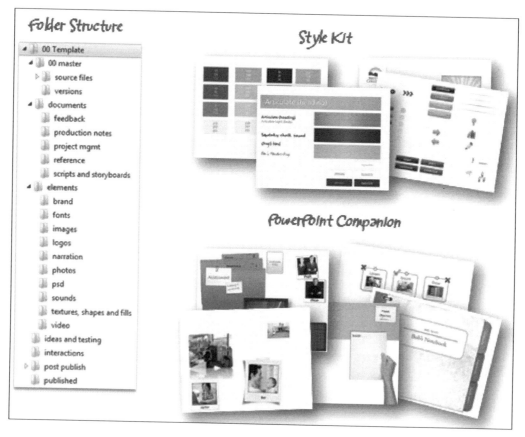

Productivity boosters

There are many ways to boost productivity when using Storyline. Your best bet will be to approach development from the point of view of what's really necessary and avoid creating more complexity than what's called for. Often the most elegant solution is the simplest one.

Top 10 Storyline productivity boosters

Here are 10 common methods to boost your productivity with Storyline:

1. Become a master formatter. This means using shortcut keys and automating where you can. Here are some examples:

    ◦   When you need to apply formatting to multiple objects over multiple layers or slides, double-click on the **Format Painter** option. This lets you to continue applying formatting until you click anywhere outside the slide.

    ◦   Need to apply a trigger to multiple objects? Copy the trigger then select all of the objects and click on the **Paste** button in the **Trigger** panel. All you need to do now is make slight adjustments to each instead of creating each trigger from scratch.

    ◦   You can also use Duplicate or *Ctrl* + *D* to quickly copy objects. For example, you might have multiple instances of the same interaction on a slide, perhaps a tabbed interaction. To set up another fully working instance, you can select all the objects that make up the interaction and then duplicate the elements and make slight adjustments. Remember that *Ctrl* + *A* is a shortcut key for selecting all of the elements on a slide.

    ◦   If you use a shape effect for a lot of the shapes in a project, such as fills, outlines, and alignment, why repeat formatting over and over again every time you insert a new shape when you can right-click on a shape, button, or caption and choose **Set as Default**. Next time you use one of these elements, it will come preformatted using your most frequently used settings.

    ◦   Size your graphics before importing them into Storyline. You want crisp, clear images. If you resize an image in Storyline, it will become fuzzy since Storyline works only with raster graphics, not scalable vector graphics. Note that the maximum size for an image in Storyline is 2048 x 2048 pixels.

○ Study the shortcut keys that are listed in the *Appendix* of this book and get in the habit of using them for most tasks. This seems minor but it will save a lot of time. It's also worthwhile to customize the **Quick Access** toolbar so that features you commonly use are just a click away.

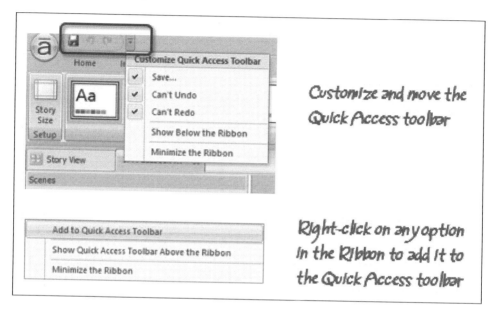

○ Place the audio and video objects in once, then copy and paste when you need to use the same clips on other slides. It's faster than importing, particularly using shortcut keys. The bonus is that Storyline does not increase the file size, it recognizes the duplicates as copies whereas importing each time increases the file size and treats each instance as a unique object, consuming memory, file space, and additional to publishing time.

2. Keep the trigger logic simple and well planned. Consistently organize them from slide-to-slide so it's easier to interpret and edit.

3. Use short variable names that are descriptive with logical sequencing and numbering. It's much easier to see short variable names in various displays and drop-down menus.

4. Get into the habit of naming the objects in the timeline, again using short names that are meaningful. This will speed up production by consuming less of your time trying to figure out which object is which.

5. Leverage templates whenever you can. There are numerous ways you can do this:

    1. Use the Save As... feature in the Articulate menu to save a projects as a Storyline template. This saves not only the look and feel, interactions and player set up, but also glossary and resource information. This is a great technique when creating multiple courses that are part of a series.

    2. If you have a single activity that you want to re-use, save it by itself in a Storyline file and then Import the slide(s) into other projects. This speeds up production time because you are re-using, not re-creating, you work with the added bonus that the interaction comes already error-free and tested.

    3. Make use of Master Slides to automate custom navigation. Set up your navigation buttons and links once on a master slide rather than duplicate on each individual slide.

6. Use cue points to synchronize animations. It's a simple feature but a time saver. Clicking on the **Play** button in the timeline plays back the slide animations and audio track. Pressing C on the keyboard creates a cue point as you listen to the audio. Later, you can align objects and animations to these markers.

7. Keep daily versions, if you're working on things daily or weekly, if it's upkeep. Use a consistent naming convention, for example, projectname-v001, -v002, and so on.

8. Preview often and publish frequently to check your progress. Look for design inconsistency issues, functional errors, and navigation problems on more than one monitor and in more than one browser. This will go a long way in catching technical or design issues early in the process, otherwise you'll have to apply changes to more slides/scenes later, which will slow down your productivity and increase your risk of errors.

9. Take the time to get to know where the limitations are with Storyline, what works well and not so well. Document tips and best practices and share it with your team. It's a continual learning process and when shared, boosts the productivity of the entire team.

10. Save your projects often. There is no autosave in Storyline.

Summary

This chapter highlighted some of the techniques you can use right away to begin boosting your productivity with Storyline.

The title of the chapter is *Rapid Development*, but this is an overused term with many meanings. It's impossible for a software tool to help you rapidly develop e-learning courses. The tool can make the process more approachable, but as a developer or instructional designer, you need to have the know-how and skills to properly operate the tool. Great e-learning always begins with great content. You can dramatically reduce production time by spending more time up-front in the planning stages finalizing content and navigation prior to starting development in Storyline.

By practicing the top 10 productivity boosters, you'll be setting yourself up to work more strategically with Storyline, where you are seeing the full potential of the tool and will be able to apply your skills with the tool to specific learning events in your courses.

As you've seen, Storyline has an almost open door policy where they have made it incredibly easy to leverage the work you've already created in other tools. By extension, you can easily curate the content you've not created; this is a huge time saver and adds a level of depth that would have taken much longer to create any other way.

One of the best ways to become more efficient and effective in Storyline is to participate in the community of developers. This particular community is very active and the Articulate *E-Learning Heroes Forums* (http://community.articulate.com/forums/) are filled to the brim with helpful tips, techniques, inspiration, and conversations. Your participation in this community will help you to become an enthusiastic Storyline expert and a seasoned e-learning developer.

Appendix

Here is a collection of tutorials, links, and ideas for inspiration to help you with your Storyline skills.

The Appendix is organized by subject matter as follows:

- The Articulate community
- Design and development
- Working with media
- Assets and templates
- Accessibility
- Inspiration

The Articulate community

Join in the conversation! Connect with the Articulate community by becoming an 'e-learning hero' at `http://community.articulate.com/`.

You'll find me there. Please feel free to reach out and connect:

`http://community.articulate.com/members/StephanieHarnett/default.aspx`

- **Email**: `slhice@stephanieharnett.ca`
- **Twitter**: `http://twitter.com/slhice`
- **Screenr**: `http://www.screenr.com/user/slhice`
- **LinkedIn**: `http://ca.linkedin.com/in/slhice`
- **Website**: `http://www.stephanieharnett.ca/` (created in Storyline)

Design and development

There is an ever growing list of tips and discussions that will help you improve your design and development techniques and processes. Check out this best practices discussion in the Articulate forums at `http://community.articulate.com/forums/p/26427/146923.aspx#146923` and chime in.

Here is a collection of some other useful links and information to refer to when designing and developing in Storyline.

Description	Link
Storyline Support	`http://www.articulate.com/support/kb.php?product=st1`
Storyline Tutorials	`http://community.articulate.com/tutorials/products/articulate-storyline.aspx`
JavaScript Examples	`http://www.articulate.com/support/kb_article.php?product=st1&id=11wes8cn32vg`
Flash & ActionScript Best Practices	`http://www.articulate.com/support/kb_article.php?product=st1&id=vw0igndn2njl`
Mind Maps for Design	`http://community.articulate.com/downloads/p/730.aspx`
5-point Makeover Methodology	`http://multimedialearning.com/` (David Anderson from Articulate)

File locations

Storyline uses various files located on your computer to control the look and feel of your projects. Knowing these locations is important, particularly if you would like to share these files with other people who are also working on Storyline projects.

 The table below references locations specific to Windows Vista or later. Windows XP locations are slightly different, with a starting path of `C:\Documents and Settings\%username%\Application Data\` instead of `\AppData\Roaming\`.

Description	Link
Design Theme	`\AppData\Roaming\Articulate\Templates\Themes\`
Theme Colors	`\AppData\Roaming\Articulate\Templates\Themes\` `Theme Colors`
Theme Fonts	`\AppData\Roaming\Articulate\Templates\Themes\` `Theme Fonts`
Theme Effects	`\AppData\Roaming\Articulate\Templates\Themes\` `Theme Effects`
Players	`\AppData\Roaming\Articulate\Shared\2.0\Players`
Custom Player Color Themes	Custom player color themes can be saved by saving the color scheme then opening it in another project.
	`\AppData\Roaming\Articulate\Shared\2.0\\` `Frames\StoryFrame\ColorSchemes`
Story Templates	`\My Articulate Projects\Storyline Templates`

Flash, HTML and mobile feature comparison

Articulate has created a table that compares features that are supported in Flash, HTML5 and the Articulate mobile player app for the iPad. You can view this compatibility table available at `http://www.articulate.com/support/kb_` `article.php?product=st1&id=1568gg1ayot2`.

Creating your own keyboard shortcuts

You can create your own keyboard shortcuts by adding features to the **Quick Access Toolbar**. All you need to do is right-click on the button for any Storyline feature, and select **Add to Quick Access Toolbar**. To use a feature with a shortcut key, press and hold the *Alt* key on the keyboard, then press the number that matches the button you want to launch. The first button on the Quick Access Toolbar is **1**, the second is **2**, and so on.

You can view a tutorial on how to do this at `http://www.screenr.com/D3Z8`.

Player color customization

The color selector in the Storyline Player lets you change the color of different parts of the Player. You can view a quick reference chart that visually depicts this and download it from Articulate at `http://community.articulate.com/downloads/p/80796.aspx`.

Story size and dimensions

An important initial consideration when creating a new project in Storyline is the Story size. This includes the actual slide size as well as the Player dimensions. You must also factor in how the course will be viewed. Here are some guidelines related to these design decisions.

Designing for multiple devices

The story size needs to be 4:3 ratio for an iPad, so the default of 720 x 540 will work, but also 1024 x 768 scaled to fill browser window. Most developers agree that a story size of 988 x 741 works well for desktop and iPad delivery. Designers may opt for a precise 978 grid system with the story size set to 988 x 643.

Common breakpoints (size limitations)

320 pixels: mobile portrait

480 pixels: mobile landscape

600 pixels: small tablet

768 pixels: tablet portrait

1024 pixels: table landscape/netbook

1280 pixels: desktop

Player size considerations

The Storyline Player adds a minimum of 10 pixels all the way around your story content when published. Depending on the features and controls you've included on your player, the player can add between 20 and 260 pixels to the width and between 20 and 118 pixels to the height.

Below are common player configurations with a 720 x 540 slide size and the associated player size and published size:

Player features	Player Size	Published Size
No features	10 pixels all around	740 x 560
Next/previous buttons	10 pixels all around + 51 pixels in height	740 x 611
Next/previous buttons Resources tab	10 pixels all around + 51 pixels in height + 24 pixels in height	740 x 635
Next/previous buttons Resources tab + Title	10 pixels all around + 51 pixels in height + 47 pixels in height	740 x 658
Next/previous buttons Resources tab + Title Side Menu	10 pixels all around + 51 pixels in height + 47 pixels in height + 240 pixels in width	980 x 658

Working with media

Here are some tips when working with media in Storyline.

Description	Link
Importing from PowerPoint	http://www.articulate.com/support/kb_article.php?product=st1&id=catmp4tjk9r8
PowerPoint Considerations	http://www.articulate.com/support/kb_article.php?product=st1&id=catmp4tjk9r8
Importing from Captivate	http://www.articulate.com/support/kb_article.php?product=st1&id=qlzslj9rue8k
Looping Audio	http://www.articulate.com/support/kb_article.php?product=st1&id=j5dv0b6lm4q3
Drag and Drop Interaction	http://www.screenr.com/iCy8
Generating Closed Captions	http://community.articulate.com/forums/p/14677/111423.aspx#111423
Create a Certificate	http://www.articulate.com/support/kb_article.php?product=st1&id=8nkon52m3h71

Assets and templates

Here are some links to various free resources that will help speed up your development.

Description	Link
Free Templates	http://community.articulate.com/downloads/g/storyline/default.aspx
Free Assets	http://community.articulate.com/downloads/
Storyline Characters	http://community.articulate.com/downloads/p/73285.aspx
Bookshelf Navigation	Demo: http://stephanieharnett.ca/guild/policy/index.html
	Source: http://stephanieharnett.ca/guild/policy/policy.story
Video Interaction	Demo: http://stephanieharnett.ca/guild/videointeraction/story.html
	Source: http://stephanieharnett.ca/guild/videointeraction/videointeraction.story
Photo Gallery	Demo:
	http://stephanieharnett.ca/screenr/gallery/story.html
	Source:
	http://stephanieharnett.ca/screenr/gallery/gallery.story
Memory Game	Demo:
	http://stephanieharnett.ca/screenr/memorygame/story.html
	Source:
	http://stephanieharnett.ca/screenr/memorygame/memorygame.story

Accessibility

Storyline offers support for people with disabilities so that they are able to use interactive e-learning courses created with Storyline, with the help of assistive software, such as the **JAWS** screen reader.

Section 508, a US Federal law, requires that all Federal agencies give disabled people access to information that is comparable to the access available to others. Storyline supports Section 508 in the following ways:

- Keyboard support
- Content focus
- Flicker reduction
- Non-visual operation and information retrieval
- Large text
- Text equivalents
- Assistive technology: Ready UI, Forms, Scripts

How Storyline complies with Section 508 is detailed on their website at `http://www.articulate.com/products/storyline-section-508-vpat.php`.

There are tips and guidelines available for Storyline developers on the Articulate website at `http://www.articulate.com/products/storyline-section-508.php`.

 Storyline does not have a built-in **Closed Captions** feature. You can add a transcript by using the **Notes** panel but this does not create true Closed Captions that follow along as the narrator speaks. A fellow Articulate "Super Hero", *Steve Flowers*, came up with a solution and provides a demonstration with source code and discussion in the Articulate forums located at `http://community.articulate.com/forums/p/14677/111423.aspx#111423`.

Inspiration

My design inspiration for e-learning comes from thoughtfully designed websites that I encounter on the web. Ideas for approaching an e-learning activity requires more focus, and for that, I often turn to these folks for ideas and inspiration:

Description	Link
Articulate Rapid e-Learning Blog	`http://www.articulate.com/rapid-elearning/`
e-Learning Examples	`http://elearningexamples.com/`
Articulate Tutorials (on Screenr)	David Anderson
	`http://www.screenr.com/user/elearning`
	Tom Kuhlmann
	`http://www.screenr.com/user/tomkuhlmann`
	Jeanette Brooks
	`http://www.screenr.com/user/jeanettebrooks`
	David Fair
	`http://www.screenr.com/user/articulatedf`
	Mike Enders
	`http://www.screenr.com/user/endersdesign`

Index

slide notes 35
working with 34
Text Entry question 190
text labels tab, Player 235
text variable 130
timeline
about 26
Notes panel 26
object appearance, controlling 28
reading 28
Timeline panel 26
viewing 26
working with 27
Tom Kuhlmann
URL 270
tracking
publishing with 243
transition
applying, to slide 50, 51
triggers
about 55, 59
copying 63
creating, steps for 62
deleting 63
duplicating 63
object triggers 59
order, changing 63
pasting 63
slide triggers 59
uses 59, 60
Trigger Wizard window 66
trim 203
True/False variable 130
Try mode
step-by-step recordings, inserting 214

V

variables
about 127-129
creating, steps for 135
formatting, adjusting 132, 133

functionality, preventing 133, 134
new project, creating 131
new slides, adding 133, 134
reference, inserting 137
setting up 146
slides, adjusting 131
types 130
using 136
variables, types
number variable 130
text variable 130
True/False variable 130
video
about 201
basic tasks 203
editing 202
editing tools 203
inserting, from website 204, 205
inserting, in story 202
pointers 224
URL 268
View mode
step-by-step recordings, inserting 213
visual help 38

W

web
publishing to 240-242
web content
about 208
adding, to story 209
Web Object icon 210
website
video, inserting from 204, 205

Z

zoom feature 219, 220

Articulate Studio Cookbook

ISBN: 978-1-84969-308-0   Paperback: 292 pages

Create traning course with Articulate Studio's strong interactivity and rich content capabilities, all within the familiarity of Microsoft PowerPoint

1. Complete your courses by creating Flash-ready presentations through familiar PowerPoint

2. Employ Articulate Engage, Quizmaker and Encoder to make dazzling interaction, asses learners and add full-motion videos

3. Practical recipes to get you moving on a specific activity without the extra fluff

Mastering Adobe Captivate 6

ISBN: 978-1-84969-244-1   Paperback: 476 pages

Create professional SCORM-compliant eLearning content with Adobe Captivate

1. Step by step tutorial to build three projects including a demonstration, a simulation and a random SCORM-compliant quiz featuring all possible question slides.

2. Enhance your projects by adding interactivity, animations, sound and more

3. Publish your project in a wide variety of formats enabling virtually any desktop and mobile devices to play your e-learning content

Please check **www.PacktPub.com** for information on our titles

WordPress for Education

ISBN: 978-1-84951-820-8   Paperback: 144 pages

Create interactive and engaging e-learning websites with WordPress

1. Develop effective e-learning websites that will engage your students

2. Extend the potential of a classroom website with WordPress plugins

3. Create an interactive social network and course management system to enhance student and instructor communication

Desire2Learn for Higher Education Cookbook

ISBN: 978-1-84969-344-8   Paperback: 206 pages

Gain expert knowledge of the tools within the Desire2Learn Learning Environment, maximize your productivity, and create online learning experiences with these easy-to-follow recipes

1. Customize the look and feel of your online course, integrate graphics and video, and become more productive using the learning environment's built-in assessment and collaboration tools

2. Recipes address real world challenges in clear and concise step-by-step instructions, which help you work your way through technical tasks with ease

3. Detailed instructions with screenshots to guide you through each task

Please check **www.PacktPub.com** for information on our titles